XML

Pocket Reference

XML
Pocket Reference

Second Edition

Robert Eckstein
with Michel Casabianca

Beijing • Cambridge • Farnham • Köln • Paris • Sebastopol • Taipei • Tokyo

XML Pocket Reference, Second Edition

by Robert Eckstein with Michel Casabianca

Published by O'Reilly & Associates, Inc., 1005 Gravenstein Highway North, Sebastopol, CA 95472.

Editor: Ellen Siever

Production Editor: Jeffrey Holcomb

Cover Designer: Hanna Dyer

Printing History:

October 1999:	First Edition
April 2001:	Second Edition

0-596-00133-9
[C] [6/03]

Table of Contents

XML Pocket Reference

Introduction

The *Extensible Markup Language* (XML) is a document-processing standard that is an official recommendation of the World Wide Web Consortium (W3C), the same group responsible for overseeing the HTML standard. Many expect XML and its sibling technologies to become the markup language of choice for dynamically generated content, including non-static web pages. Many companies are already integrating XML support into their products.

XML is actually a simplified form of *Standard Generalized Markup Language* (SGML), an international documentation standard that has existed since the 1980s. However, SGML is extremely complex, especially for the Web. Much of the credit for XML's creation can be attributed to Jon Bosak of Sun Microsystems, Inc., who started the W3C working group responsible for scaling down SGML to a form more suitable for the Internet.

Put succinctly, XML is a *meta language* that allows you to create and format your own document markups. With HTML, existing markup is static: `<HEAD>` and `<BODY>`, for example, are tightly integrated into the HTML standard and cannot be changed or extended. XML, on the other hand, allows you to create your own markup tags and configure each to your liking—for example, `<HeadingA>`, `<Sidebar>`, `<Quote>`, or `<Really-WildFont>`. Each of these elements can be defined through your own *document type definitions* and *stylesheets* and applied to one or more XML documents. XML schemas provide another way to define elements. Thus, it is important to realize that there are no "correct" tags for an XML document, except those you define yourself.

While many XML applications currently support *Cascading Style Sheets* (CSS), a more extensible stylesheet specification exists, called the *Extensible Stylesheet Language* (XSL). With XSL, you ensure that XML documents are formatted the same way no matter which application or platform they appear on.

XSL consists of two parts: XSLT (*transformations*) and XSL-FO (*formatting objects*). Transformations, as discussed in this book, allow you to work with XSLT and convert XML documents to other formats such as HTML. Formatting objects are described briefly in the section "Formatting Objects."

This book offers a quick overview of XML, as well as some sample applications that allow you to get started in coding. We won't cover everything about XML. Some XML-related specifications are still in flux as this book goes to print. However, after reading this book, we hope that the components that make up XML will seem a little less foreign.

XML Terminology

Before we move further, we need to standardize some terminology. An XML document consists of one or more *elements*. An element is marked with the following form:

```
<Body>
This is text formatted according to the Body element
</Body>.
```

This element consists of two *tags*: an opening tag, which places the name of the element between a less-than sign (<) and a greater-than sign (>), and a closing tag, which is identical except for the forward slash (/) that appears before the element name. Like HTML, the text between the opening and closing tags is considered part of the element and is processed according to the element's rules.

Elements can have *attributes* applied, such as the following:

```
<Price currency="Euro">25.43</Price>
```

Here, the attribute is specified inside of the opening tag and is called `currency`. It is given a value of `Euro`, which is placed inside quotation marks. Attributes are often used to further refine or modify the default meaning of an element.

In addition to the standard elements, XML also supports *empty elements*. An empty element has no text between the opening and closing tags. Hence, both tags can (optionally) be combined by placing a forward slash before the closing marker. For example, these elements are identical:

```
<Picture src="blueball.gif"></Picture>
<Picture src="blueball.gif"/>
```

Empty elements are often used to add nontextual content to a document or provide additional information to the application that parses the XML. Note that while the closing slash may not be used in single-tag HTML elements, it is *mandatory* for single-tag XML empty elements.

Unlearning Bad Habits

Whereas HTML browsers often ignore simple errors in documents, XML applications are not nearly as forgiving. For the HTML reader, there are a few bad habits from which we should dissuade you:

XML is case-sensitive
: Element names must be used exactly as they are defined. For example, `<Paragraph>` and `<paragraph>` are not the same.

Attribute values must be in quotation marks
: You can't specify an attribute value as `<picture src=/images/blueball.gif/>`, an error that HTML browsers often overlook. An attribute value must always be inside

single or double quotation marks, or else the XML parser will flag it as an error. Here is the correct way to specify such a tag:

```
<picture src="/images/blueball.gif"/>
```

A non-empty element must have an opening and a closing tag

Each element that specifies an opening tag must have a closing tag that matches it. If it does not, and it is not an empty element, the XML parser generates an error. In other words, you cannot do the following:

```
<Paragraph>
This is a paragraph.
<Paragraph>
This is another paragraph.
```

Instead, you must have an opening and a closing tag for each paragraph element:

```
<Paragraph>This is a paragraph.</Paragraph>
<Paragraph>This is another paragraph.</Paragraph>
```

Tags must be nested correctly

It is illegal to do the following:

```
<Italic><Bold>This is incorrect</Italic></Bold>
```

The closing tag for the `<Bold>` element should be inside the closing tag for the `<Italic>` element to match the nearest opening tag and preserve the correct element nesting. It is essential for the application parsing your XML to process the hierarchy of the elements:

```
<Italic><Bold>This is correct</Bold></Italic>
```

These syntactic rules are the source of many common errors in XML, especially because some of this behavior can be ignored by HTML browsers. An XML document adhering to these rules (and a few others that we'll see later) is said to be *well-formed.*

An Overview of an XML Document

Generally, two files are needed by an XML-compliant application to use XML content:

The XML document
: This file contains the document data, typically tagged with meaningful XML elements, any of which may contain attributes.

Document Type Definition (DTD)
: This file specifies rules for how the XML elements, attributes, and other data are defined and logically related in the document.

Additionally, another type of file is commonly used to help display XML data: the *stylesheet.*

The stylesheet dictates how document elements should be formatted when they are displayed. Note that you can apply different stylesheets to the same document, depending on the environment, thus changing the document's appearance without affecting any of the underlying data. The separation between content and formatting is an important distinction in XML.

A Simple XML Document

Example 1 shows a simple XML document.

Example 1. sample.xml

```
<?xml version="1.0" encoding="UTF-8"?>
<!DOCTYPE OReilly:Books SYSTEM "sample.dtd">
<!-- Here begins the XML data -->
<OReilly:Books xmlns:OReilly='http://www.oreilly.com'>
   <OReilly:Product>XML Pocket Reference</OReilly:Product>
   <OReilly:Price>12.95</OReilly:Price>
</OReilly:Books>
```

Let's look at this example line by line.

In the first line, the code between the `<?xml` and the `?>` is called an XML declaration. This declaration contains special information for the XML processor (the program reading the XML), indicating that this document conforms to Version 1.0 of the XML standard and uses UTF-8 (Unicode optimized for ASCII) encoding.

The second line is as follows:

```
<!DOCTYPE OReilly:Books SYSTEM "sample.dtd">
```

This line points out the *root element* of the document, as well as the DTD validating each of the document elements that appear inside the root element. The root element is the outermost element in the document that the DTD applies to; it typically denotes the document's starting and ending point. In this example, the `<OReilly:Books>` element serves as the root element of the document. The `SYSTEM` keyword denotes that the DTD of the document resides in an external file named *sample.dtd.* On a side note, it is possible to simply embed the DTD in the same file as the XML document. However, this is not recommended for general use because it hampers reuse of DTDs.

Following that line is a comment. Comments always begin with `<!--` and end with `-->`. You can write whatever you want inside comments; they are ignored by the XML processor. Be aware that comments, however, cannot come before the XML declaration and cannot appear inside an element tag. For example, this is illegal:

```
<OReilly:Books <!-- This is the tag for a book -->>
```

Finally, the elements `<OReilly:Product>`, `<OReilly:Price>`, and `<OReilly:Books>` are XML elements we invented. Like most elements in XML, they hold no special significance except for whatever document rules we define for them. Note that these elements look slightly different than those you may have seen previously because we are using namespaces. Each element tag can be divided into two parts. The portion before the colon (:) identifies the tag's namespace; the portion after the colon identifies the name of the tag itself.

Let's discuss some XML terminology. The `<OReilly:Product>` and `<OReilly:Price>` elements would both consider the `<OReilly:Books>` element their *parent.* In the same manner, elements can be *grandparents* and *grandchildren* of other elements. However, we typically abbreviate multiple levels by stating that an element is either an *ancestor* or a *descendant* of another element.

Namespaces

Namespaces were created to ensure uniqueness among XML elements. They are not mandatory in XML, but it's often wise to use them.

For example, let's pretend that the `<OReilly:Books>` element was simply named `<Books>`. When you think about it, it's not out of the question that another publisher would create its own `<Books>` element in its own XML documents. If the two publishers combined their documents, resolving a single (correct) definition for the `<Books>` tag would be impossible. When two XML documents containing identical elements from different sources are merged, those elements are said to *collide.* Namespaces help to avoid element collisions by scoping each tag.

In Example 1, we scoped each tag with the `OReilly` namespace. Namespaces are declared using the `xmlns:`*`something`* attribute, where *`something`* defines the prefix of the namespace. The attribute value is a unique identifier that differentiates this namespace from all other namespaces; the use of a URI is recommended. In this case, we use the O'Reilly URI *http://www.oreilly.com* as the default namespace, which should guarantee uniqueness. A namespace declaration can appear as an attribute of any element, in which case the namespace remains inside that element's opening and closing tags. Here are some examples:

```
<OReilly:Books xmlns:OReilly='http://www.oreilly.com'>
  ...
</OReilly:Books>
```

```
<xsl:stylesheet xmlns:xsl='http://www.w3.org'>
  ...
</xsl:stylesheet>
```

You are allowed to define more than one namespace in the context of an element:

```
<OReilly:Books xmlns:OReilly='http://www.oreilly.com'
    xmlns:Songline='http://www.songline.com'>
  ...
</OReilly:Books>
```

If you do not specify a name after the xmlns prefix, the namespace is dubbed the *default namespace* and is applied to all elements inside the defining element that do not use a namespace prefix of their own. For example:

```
<Books xmlns='http://www.oreilly.com'
      xmlns:Songline='http://www.songline.com'>
    <Book>
        <Title>XML Pocket Reference</Title>
        <ISBN>0-596-00133-9</ISBN>
    </Book>
    <Songline:CD>18231</Songline:CD>
</Books>
```

Here, the default namespace (represented by the URI *http://www.oreilly.com*) is applied to the elements <Books>, <Book>, <Title>, and <ISBN>. However, it is not applied to the <Songline:CD> element, which has its own namespace.

Finally, you can set the default namespace to an empty string. This ensures that there is no default namespace in use within a specific element:

```
<header xmlns=''
        xmlns:OReilly='http://www.oreilly.com'
        xmlns:Songline='http://www.songline.com'>
   <entry>Learn XML in a Week</entry>
   <price>10.00</price>
</header>
```

Here, the <entry> and <price> elements have no default namespace.

A Simple Document Type Definition (DTD)

Example 2 creates a simple DTD for our XML document.

Example 2. sample.dtd

```
<?xml version="1.0"?>
<!ELEMENT OReilly:Books (OReilly:Product, OReilly:Price)>
<!ATTLIST OReilly:Books
        xmlns:OReilly CDATA "http://www.oreilly.com">
<!ELEMENT OReilly:Product (#PCDATA)>
<!ELEMENT OReilly:Price (#PCDATA)>
```

The purpose of this DTD is to declare each of the elements used in our XML document. All document-type data is placed inside a construct with the characters `<!something>`.

Each `<!ELEMENT>` construct declares a valid element for our XML document. With the second line, we've specified that the `<OReilly:Books>` element is valid:

```
<!ELEMENT OReilly:Books
   (OReilly:Product, OReilly:Price)>
```

The parentheses group together the required child elements for the element `<OReilly:Books>`. In this case, the `<OReilly:Product>` and `<OReilly:Price>` elements *must* be included inside our `<OReilly:Books>` element tags, and they must appear in the order specified. The elements `<OReilly:Product>` and `<OReilly:Price>` are therefore considered *children* of `<OReilly:Books>`.

Likewise, the `<OReilly:Product>` and `<OReilly:Price>` elements are declared in our DTD:

```
<!ELEMENT OReilly:Product (#PCDATA)>
<!ELEMENT OReilly:Price (#PCDATA)>
```

Again, parentheses specify required elements. In this case, they both have a single requirement, represented by `#PCDATA`. This is shorthand for *parsed character data*, which means that any characters are allowed, as long as they do not include other element tags or contain the characters < or &, or the sequence]]>. These characters are forbidden because they could be interpreted as markup. (We'll see how to get around this shortly.)

The line `<!ATTLIST OReilly:Books xmlns:OReilly CDATA "http://www.oreilly.com">` indicates that the `<xmlns:OReilly>` attribute of the `<OReilly:Books>` element defaults to the URI associated with O'Reilly & Associates if no other value is explicitly specified in the element.

The XML data shown in Example 1 adheres to the rules of this DTD: it contains an `<OReilly:Books>` element, which in turn contains an `<OReilly:Product>` element followed by an `<OReilly:Price>` element inside it (in that order). Therefore, if this DTD is applied to the data with a `<!DOCTYPE>` statement, the document is said to be *valid*.

A Simple XSL Stylesheet

XSL allows developers to describe transformations using XSL Transformations (XSLT), which can convert XML documents into XSL Formatting Objects, HTML, or other textual output.

As this book goes to print, the XSL Formatting Objects specification is still changing; therefore, this book covers only the XSLT portion of XSL. The examples that follow, however, are consistent with the W3C specification.

Let's add a simple XSL stylesheet to the example:

```
<?xml version="1.0"?>
<xsl:stylesheet version="1.0"
    xmlns:xsl="http://www.w3.org/1999/XSL/Transform">
    <xsl:output method="html"/>
    <xsl:template match="/">
        <font size="+1">
            <xsl:apply-templates/>
        </font>
    </xsl:template>
</xsl:stylesheet>
```

The first thing you might notice when you look at an XSL stylesheet is that it is formatted in the same way as a regular XML document. This is not a coincidence. By design, XSL stylesheets are themselves XML documents, so they must adhere to the same rules as well-formed XML documents.

Breaking down the pieces, you should first note that all XSL elements must be contained in the appropriate `<xsl:stylesheet>` outer element. This tells the XSLT processor that it is describing stylesheet information, not XML content itself. After the opening `<xsl:stylesheet>` tag, we see an XSLT directive to optimize output for HTML. Following that are the rules that will be applied to our XML document, given by the `<xsl:template>` elements (in this case, there is only one rule).

Each rule can be further broken down into two items: a *template pattern* and a *template action.* Consider the line:

```
<xsl:template match="/">
```

This line forms the template pattern of the stylesheet rule. Here, the target pattern is the root element, as designated by `match="/"`. The `/` is shorthand to represent the XML document's root element.

The contents of the `<xsl:template>` element:

```
<font size="+1">
    <xsl:apply-templates/>
</font>
```

specify the template action that should be performed on the target. In this case, we see the empty element `<xsl:apply-templates/>` located inside a `<font>` element. When the XSLT processor transforms the target element, every element inside the root element is surrounded by the `<font>` tags, which will likely cause the application formatting the output to increase the font size.

In our initial XML example, the `<OReilly:Product>` and `<OReilly:Price>` elements are both enclosed inside the `<OReilly:Books>` tags. Therefore, the font size will be applied to the contents of those tags. Example 3 displays a more realistic example.

Example 3. sample.xsl

```
<?xml version="1.0"?>
<xsl:stylesheet version="1.0"
   xmlns:xsl="http://www.w3c.org/1999/XSL/Transform"
   xmlns:OReilly="http://www.oreilly.com">

   <xsl:output method="html">

   <xsl:template match="/">
      <html>
         <body>
            <xsl:apply-templates/>
         </body>
      </html>
   </xsl:template>

   <xsl:template match="OReilly:Books">
      <font size="+3">
         <xsl:text>Books: </xsl:text>
         <br/>
            <xsl:apply-templates/>
      </font>
   </xsl:template>

   <xsl:template match="OReilly:Product">
      <font size="+0">
         <xsl:apply-templates/>
         <br/>
      </font>
   </xsl:template>

   <xsl:template match="OReilly:Price">
      <font size="+1">
         <xsl:text>Price: $</xsl:text>
            <xsl:apply-templates/>
         <xsl:text> + tax</xsl:text>
         <br/>
      </font>
   </xsl:template>
</xsl:stylesheet>
```

In this example, we target the `<OReilly:Books>` element, printing the word `Books:` before it in a larger font size. In addition, the `<OReilly:Product>` element applies the default font size to each of its children, and the `<OReilly:Price>` tag uses a slightly larger font size to display its children, overriding the default size of its parent, `<OReilly:Books>`. (Of course, neither one has any children elements; they simply have text between their tags in the XML document.) The text `Price: $` will precede each of `<OReilly:Price>`'s children, and the characters `+ tax` will come after it, formatted accordingly.

Here is the result after we pass *sample.xsl* through an XSLT processor:

```
<html xmlns:OReilly="http://www.oreilly.com">
   <body>
      <font size="+3">
   Books: <br>
         <font size="+0">
XML Pocket Reference<br>
         </font>
         <font size="+1">
Price $12.95 + tax
         </font>
      </font>
   </body>
</html>
```

And that's it: everything needed for a simple XML document! Running the result through an HTML browser, you should see something similar to Figure 1.

XML Reference

Now that you have had a quick taste of working with XML, here is an overview of the more common rules and constructs of the XML language.

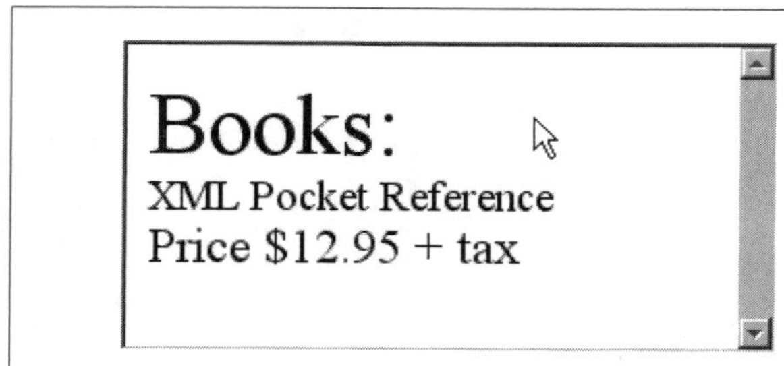

Figure 1. Sample XML output

Well-Formed XML

These are the rules for a well-formed XML document:

- All element attribute values must be in quotation marks.
- An element must have both an opening and a closing tag, unless it is an empty element.
- If a tag is a standalone empty element, it must contain a closing slash (/) before the end of the tag.
- All opening and closing element tags must nest correctly.
- Isolated markup characters are not allowed in text; < or & must use entity references. In addition, the sequence]]> must be expressed as]]> when used as regular text. (Entity references are discussed in further detail later.)
- Well-formed XML documents without a corresponding DTD must have all attributes of type CDATA by default.

Special Markup

XML uses the following special markup constructs.

<?xml . . . ?>

```
<?xml version="number"
[encoding="encoding"]
[standalone="yes|no"] ?>
```

Although they are not required to, XML documents typically begin with an XML declaration, which must start with the characters `<?xml` and end with the characters `?>`. Attributes include:

`version`
: The `version` attribute specifies the correct version of XML required to process the document, which is currently `1.0`. This attribute cannot be omitted.

`encoding`
: The `encoding` attribute specifies the character encoding used in the document (e.g., `UTF-8` or `iso-8859-1`). UTF-8 and UTF-16 are the only encodings that an XML processor is required to handle. This attribute is optional.

`standalone`
: The optional `standalone` attribute specifies whether an external DTD is required to parse the document. The value must be either `yes` or `no` (the default). If the value is `no` or the attribute is not present, a DTD must be declared with an XML `<!DOCTYPE>` instruction. If it is `yes`, no external DTD is required.

For example:

```
<?xml version="1.0"?>
<?xml version="1.0" encoding="UTF-8" standalone="yes"?>
```

<?...?>

```
<?target attribute1="value"
attribute2="value"
... ?>
```

A processing instruction allows developers to place attributes specific to an outside application within the document. Processing instructions always begin with the characters `<?` and end with the characters `?>`. For example:

```
<?works document="hello.doc" data="hello.wks"?>
```

You can create your own processing instructions if the XML application processing the document is aware of what the data means and acts accordingly.

<!DOCTYPE>

```
<!DOCTYPE root-element SYSTEM|PUBLIC
["name"] "URI_of_DTD">
```

The `<!DOCTYPE>` instruction allows you to specify a DTD for an XML document. This instruction currently takes one of two forms:

```
<!DOCTYPE root-element SYSTEM "URI_of_DTD">
<!DOCTYPE root-element PUBLIC "name" "URI_of_DTD">
```

`SYSTEM`
: The `SYSTEM` variant specifies the URI location of a DTD for private use in the document. For example:

```
<!DOCTYPE Book SYSTEM
  "http://mycompany.com/dtd/mydoctype.dtd">
```

`PUBLIC`
: The `PUBLIC` variant is used in situations in which a DTD has been publicized for widespread use. In these cases, the DTD is assigned a unique name, which the XML processor may use by itself to attempt to retrieve the DTD. If this fails, the URI is used:

```
<!DOCTYPE Book PUBLIC "-//O'Reilly//DTD//EN"
  "http://www.oreilly.com/dtd/xmlbk.dtd">
```

Public DTDs follow a specific naming convention. See the XML specification for details on naming public DTDs.

<!-- ... -->

```
<!-- comments -->
```

You can place comments anywhere in an XML document, except within element tags or before the initial XML processing instructions. Comments in an XML document always start with the characters <!-- and end with the characters -->. In addition, they may not include double hyphens within the comment. The contents of the comment are ignored by the XML processor. For example:

```
<!-- Sales Figures Start Here -->
<Units>2000</Units>
<Cost>49.95</Cost>
```

CDATA

```
<![CDATA[ ... ]]>
```

You can define special sections of character data, or CDATA, which the XML processor does not attempt to interpret as markup. Anything included inside a CDATA section is treated as plain text. CDATA sections begin with the characters `<![CDATA[` and end with the characters `]]>`. For example:

```
<![CDATA[
   I'm now discussing the <element> tag of documents
   5 & 6: "Sales" and "Profit and Loss". Luckily,
   the XML processor won't apply rules of formatting
   to these sentences!
]]>
```

Note that entity references inside a CDATA section will not be expanded.

Element and Attribute Rules

An element is either bound by its start and end tags or is an empty element. Elements can contain text, other elements, or a combination of both. For example:

```
<para>
   Elements can contain text, other elements, or
   a combination. For example, a chapter might
   contain a title and multiple paragraphs, and
   a paragraph might contain text and
   <emphasis>emphasis elements</emphasis>.
</para>
```

An element name must start with a letter or an underscore. It can then have any number of letters, numbers, hyphens, periods, or underscores in its name. Elements are *case-sensitive*: `<Para>`, `<para>`, and `<pArA>` are considered three different element types.

Element type names may not start with the string `xml` in any variation of upper- or lowercase. Names beginning with `xml` are reserved for special uses by the W3C XML Working Group. Colons (`:`) are permitted in element type names only for specifying namespaces; otherwise, colons are forbidden. For example:

Example	Comment
`<Italic>`	Legal
`<_Budget>`	Legal
`<Punch line>`	Illegal: has a space
`<205Para>`	Illegal: starts with number
`<repair@log>`	Illegal: contains `@` character
`<xmlbob>`	Illegal: starts with `xml`

Element type names can also include accented Roman characters, letters from other alphabets (e.g., Cyrillic, Greek, Hebrew, Arabic, Thai, Hiragana, Katakana, or Devanagari), and ideograms from the Chinese, Japanese, and Korean languages. Valid element type names can therefore include `<são>`, `<peut-être>`, `<più>`, and `<niño>`, plus a number of others our publishing system isn't equipped to handle.

If you use a DTD, the content of an element is constrained by its DTD declaration. Better XML applications inform you which elements and attributes can appear inside a specific element. Otherwise, you should check the element declaration in the DTD to determine the exact semantics.

Attributes describe additional information about an element. They always consist of a name and a value, as follows:

```
<price currency="Euro">
```

The attribute value is always quoted, using either single or double quotes. Attribute names are subject to the same restrictions as element type names.

XML Reserved Attributes

The following are reserved attributes in XML.

---

xml:lang

```
xml:lang="iso_639_identifier"
```

The `xml:lang` attribute can be used on any element. Its value indicates the language of the body of the element. This is useful in a multilingual context. For example, you might have:

```
<para xml:lang="en">Hello</para>
<para xml:lang="fr">Bonjour</para>
```

This format allows you to display one element or the other, depending on the user's language preference.

The syntax of the `xml:lang` value is defined by ISO-639. A two-letter language code is optionally followed by a hyphen and a two-letter country code. Traditionally, the language is given in lowercase and the country in uppercase (and for safety, this rule should be followed), but processors are expected to use the values in a case-insensitive manner.

In addition, ISO-3166 provides extensions for nonstandardized languages or language variants. Valid `xml:lang` values include notations such as `en`, `en-US`, `en-UK`, `en-cockney`, `i-navajo`, and `x-minbari`.

xml:space

```
xml:space="default|preserve"
```

The `xml:space` attribute indicates whether any whitespace inside the element is significant and should not be altered by the XML processor. The attribute can take one of two enumerated values:

`preserve`
: The XML application preserves all whitespace (newlines, spaces, and tabs) present within the element.

`default`
: The XML processor uses its default processing rules when deciding to preserve or discard the whitespace inside the element.

You should set `xml:space` to `preserve` only if you want an element to behave like the HTML `<pre>` element, such as when it documents source code.

Entity and Character References

Entity references are used as substitutions for specific characters (or any string substitution) in XML. A common use for entity references is to denote document symbols that might otherwise be mistaken for markup by an XML processor. XML predefines five entity references for you, which are substitutions for basic markup symbols. However, you can define as many entity references as you like in your own DTD. (See the next section.)

Entity references always begin with an ampersand (`&`) and end with a semicolon (`;`). They cannot appear inside a CDATA section but can be used anywhere else. Predefined entities in XML are shown in the following table:

Entity	Char	Notes
`&`	&	Do not use inside processing instructions.
`<`	<	Use inside attribute values quoted with ".
`>`	>	Use after]] in normal text and inside processing instructions.
`"`	"	Use inside attribute values quoted with ".
`'`	'	Use inside attribute values quoted with '.

In addition, you can provide character references for Unicode characters with a numeric character reference. A decimal character reference consists of the string `&#`, followed by the decimal number representing the character, and finally, a semicolon (;). For hexadecimal character references, the string `&#x` is followed first by the hexadecimal number representing the character and then a semicolon. For example, to represent the copyright character, you could use either of the following lines:

```
This document is &#169; 2001 by O'Reilly and Assoc.
This document is &#xA9; 2001 by O'Reilly and Assoc.
```

The character reference is replaced with the "circled-C" (©) copyright character when the document is formatted.

Document Type Definitions

A DTD specifies how elements inside an XML document should relate to each other. It also provides grammar rules for the document and each of its elements. A document adhering to the XML specifications and the rules outlined by its DTD is considered to be *valid*. (Don't confuse this with a well-formed document, which adheres only to the XML syntax rules outlined earlier.)

Element Declarations

You must declare each of the elements that appear inside your XML document within your DTD. You can do so with the `<!ELEMENT>` declaration, which uses this format:

```
<!ELEMENT elementname rule>
```

This declares an XML element and an associated rule called a *content model*, which relates the element logically to the XML document. The element name should not include `< >` characters. An element name must start with a letter or an underscore. After that, it can have any number of letters, numbers, hyphens, periods, or underscores in its name. Element names may not start with the string `xml` in any variation of upper- or lowercase. You can use a colon in element names only if you use namespaces; otherwise, it is forbidden.

ANY and PCDATA

The simplest element declaration states that between the opening and closing tags of the element, anything can appear:

```
<!ELEMENT library ANY>
```

The `ANY` keyword allows you to include other valid tags and general character data within the element. However, you may want to specify a situation where you want only general characters to appear. This type of data is better known as *parsed character data*, or PCDATA. You can specify that an element contain only PCDATA with a declaration such as the following:

```
<!ELEMENT title (#PCDATA)>
```

Remember, this declaration means that any character data that is *not* an element can appear between the element tags.

Therefore, it's legal to write the following in your XML document:

```
<title></title>
<title>XML Pocket Reference</title>
<title>Java Network Programming</title>
```

However, the following is illegal with the previous PCDATA declaration:

```
<title>
XML <emphasis>Pocket Reference</emphasis>
</title>
```

On the other hand, you may want to specify that another element *must* appear between the two tags specified. You can do this by placing the name of the element in the parentheses. The following two rules state that a <books> element must contain a <title> element, and a <title> element must contain parsed character data (or null content) but not another element:

```
<!ELEMENT books (title)>
<!ELEMENT title (#PCDATA)>
```

Multiple sequences

If you wish to dictate that multiple elements must appear in a specific order between the opening and closing tags of a specific element, you can use a comma (,) to separate the two instances:

```
<!ELEMENT books (title, authors)>
<!ELEMENT title (#PCDATA)>
<!ELEMENT authors (#PCDATA)>
```

In the preceding declaration, the DTD states that within the opening <books> and closing </books> tags, there must first appear a <title> element consisting of parsed character data. It must be immediately followed by an <authors> element containing parsed character data. The <authors> element cannot precede the <title> element.

Here is a valid XML document for the DTD excerpt defined previously:

```
<books>
   <title>XML Pocket Reference, Second Edition</title>
   <authors>Robert Eckstein with Michel Casabianca</authors>
</books>
```

The previous example showed how to specify both elements in a declaration. You can just as easily specify that one or the other appear (but not both) by using the vertical bar (|):

```
<!ELEMENT books (title|authors)>
<!ELEMENT title (#PCDATA)>
<!ELEMENT authors (#PCDATA)>
```

This declaration states that either a `<title>` element or an `<authors>` element can appear inside the `<books>` element. Note that it must have one or the other. If you omit both elements or include both elements, the XML document is not considered valid. You can, however, use a recurrence operator to allow such an element to appear more than once. Let's talk about that now.

Grouping and recurrence

You can nest parentheses inside your declarations to give finer granularity to the syntax you're specifying. For example, the following DTD states that inside the `<books>` element, the XML document must contain either a `<description>` element or a `<title>` element immediately followed by an `<author>` element. All three elements must consist of parsed character data:

```
<!ELEMENT books ((title, author)|description)>
<!ELEMENT title (#PCDATA)>
<!ELEMENT author (#PCDATA)>
<!ELEMENT description (#PCDATA)>
```

Now for the fun part: you are allowed to dictate inside an element declaration whether a single element (or a grouping of elements contained inside parentheses) must appear zero or one times, one or more times, or zero or more times. The characters used for this appear immediately after the target element (or element grouping) that they refer to and should be familiar to Unix shell programmers. Occurrence operators are shown in the following table:

Attribute	Description
?	Must appear once or not at all (zero or one times)
+	Must appear at least once (one or more times)
*	May appear any number of times or not at all (zero or more times)

If you want to provide finer granularity to the `<author>` element, you can redefine the following in the DTD:

```
<!ELEMENT author (authorname+)>
<!ELEMENT authorname (#PCDATA)>
```

This indicates that the `<author>` element must have at least one `<authorname>` element under it. It is allowed to have more than one as well. You can define more complex relationships with parentheses:

```
<!ELEMENT reviews (rating, synopsis?, comments+)*>
<!ELEMENT rating ((tutorial|reference)*, overall)>
<!ELEMENT synopsis (#PCDATA)>
<!ELEMENT comments (#PCDATA)>
<!ELEMENT tutorial (#PCDATA)>
<!ELEMENT reference (#PCDATA)>
<!ELEMENT overall (#PCDATA)>
```

Mixed content

Using the rules of grouping and recurrence to their fullest allows you to create very useful elements that contain *mixed content*. Elements with mixed content contain child elements that can intermingle with PCDATA. The most obvious example of this is a paragraph:

```
<para>
This is a <emphasis>paragraph</emphasis> element. It
contains this <link ref="http://www.w3.org">link</link>
to the W3C. Their website is <emphasis>very</emphasis>
helpful.
</para>
```

Mixed content declarations look like this:

```
<!ELEMENT quote (#PCDATA|name|joke|soundbite)*>
```

This declaration allows a `<quote>` element to contain text (#PCDATA), `<name>` elements, `<joke>` elements, and/or `<soundbite>` elements in any order. You can't specify things such as:

```
<!ELEMENT memo (#PCDATA, from, #PCDATA, to, content)>
```

Once you include `#PCDATA` in a declaration, any following elements must be separated by "or" bars (|), and the grouping must be optional and repeatable (*).

Empty elements

You must also declare each of the empty elements that can be used inside a valid XML document. This can be done with the `EMPTY` keyword:

```
<!ELEMENT elementname EMPTY>
```

For example, the following declaration defines an element in the XML document that can be used as `<statuscode/>` or `<statuscode></statuscode>`:

```
<!ELEMENT statuscode EMPTY>
```

Entities

Inside a DTD, you can declare an *entity*, which allows you to use an *entity reference* to substitute a series of characters for another character in an XML document—similar to macros.

General entities

A *general entity* is an entity that can substitute other characters inside the XML document. The declaration for a general entity uses the following format:

```
<!ENTITY name "replacement_characters">
```

We have already seen five general entity references, one for each of the characters `<`, `>`, `&`, `'`, and `"`. Each of these can be used inside an XML document to prevent the XML processor from interpreting the characters as markup. (Incidentally, you do not need to declare these in your DTD; they are always provided for you.)

Earlier, we provided an entity reference for the copyright character. We could declare such an entity in the DTD with the following:

```
<!ENTITY copyright "&#xA9;">
```

Again, we have tied the **`©right;`** entity to Unicode value 169 (or hexadecimal 0xA9), which is the “circled-C” (©) copyright character. You can then use the following in your XML document:

```
<copyright>
&copyright; 2001 by MyCompany, Inc.
</copyright>
```

There are a couple of restrictions to declaring entities:

- You cannot make circular references in the declarations. For example, the following is invalid:

  ```
  <!ENTITY entitya "&entityb; is really neat!">
  <!ENTITY entityb "&entitya; is also really neat!">
  ```

- You cannot substitute nondocument text in a DTD with a general entity reference. The general entity reference is resolved only in an XML document, not a DTD document. (If you wish to have an entity reference resolved in the DTD, you must instead use a *parameter entity reference*.)

Parameter entities

Parameter entity references appear only in DTDs and are replaced by their entity definitions in the DTD. All parameter entity references begin with a percent sign, which denotes that they cannot be used in an XML document—only in the DTD in which they are defined. Here is how to define a parameter entity:

```
<!ENTITY % name "replacement_characters">
```

Here are some examples using parameter entity references:

```
<!ENTITY % pcdata "(#PCDATA)">
<!ELEMENT authortitle %pcdata;>
```

As with general entity references, you cannot make circular references in declarations. In addition, parameter entity references must be declared before they can be used.

External entities

XML allows you to declare an *external entity* with the following syntax:

```
<!ENTITY quotes SYSTEM
      "http://www.oreilly.com/stocks/quotes.xml">
```

This allows you to copy the XML content (located at the specified URI) into the current XML document using an external entity reference. For example:

```
<document>
   <heading>Current Stock Quotes</heading>
   &quotes;
</document>
```

This example copies the XML content located at the URI *http://www.oreilly.com/stocks/quotes.xml* into the document when it's run through the XML processor. As you might guess, this works quite well when dealing with dynamic data.

Unparsed entities

By the same token, you can use an *unparsed entity* to declare non-XML content in an XML document. For example, if you want to declare an outside image to be used inside an XML document, you can specify the following in the DTD:

```
<!ENTITY image1 SYSTEM
     "http://www.oreilly.com/ora.gif" NDATA GIF89a>
```

Note that we also specify the `NDATA` (notation data) keyword, which tells exactly what type of unparsed entity the XML processor is dealing with. You typically use an unparsed entity reference as the value of an element's attribute, one defined in the DTD with the type `ENTITY` or `ENTITIES`. Here is how you should use the unparsed entity declared previously:

```
<image src="image1"/>
```

Note that we did not use an ampersand (&) or a semicolon (;). These are only used with parsed entities.

Notations

Finally, *notations* are used in conjunction with unparsed entities. A notation declaration simply matches the value of an `NDATA` keyword (`GIF89a` in our example) with more specific information. Applications are free to use or ignore this information as they see fit:

```
<!NOTATION GIF89a SYSTEM "-//CompuServe//NOTATION
     Graphics Interchange Format 89a//EN">
```

Attribute Declarations in the DTD

Attributes for various XML elements must be specified in the DTD. You can specify each of the attributes with the `<!ATTLIST>` declaration, which uses the following form:

```
<!ATTLIST target_element attr_name attr_type default>
```

The <!ATTLIST> declaration consists of the target element name, the name of the attribute, its datatype, and any default value you want to give it.

Here are some examples of legal <!ATTLIST> declarations:

```
<!ATTLIST box length CDATA "0">
<!ATTLIST box width CDATA "0">
<!ATTLIST frame visible (true|false) "true">
<!ATTLIST person marital
    (single | married | divorced | widowed) #IMPLIED>
```

In these examples, the first keyword after ATTLIST declares the name of the target element (i.e., <box>, <frame>, <person>). This is followed by the name of the attribute (i.e., length, width, visible, marital). This, in turn, is generally followed by the datatype of the attribute and its default value.

Attribute modifiers

Let's look at the default value first. You can specify any default value allowed by the specified datatype. This value must appear as a quoted string. If a default value is not appropriate, you can specify one of the modifiers listed in the following table in its place:

Modifier	Description
#REQUIRED	The attribute value must be specified with the element.
#IMPLIED	The attribute value is unspecified, to be determined by the application.
#FIXED "*value*"	The attribute value is fixed and cannot be changed by the user.
"*value*"	The default value of the attribute.

With the #IMPLIED keyword, the value can be omitted from the XML document. The XML parser must notify the application, which can take whatever action it deems appropriate at that point. With the #FIXED keyword, you must specify the default value immediately afterwards:

```
<!ATTLIST date year CDATA #FIXED "2001">
```

Datatypes

The following table lists legal datatypes to use in a DTD:

Type	Description
CDATA	Character data
enumerated	A series of values from which only one can be chosen
ENTITY	An entity declared in the DTD
ENTITIES	Multiple whitespace-separated entities declared in the DTD
ID	A unique element identifier
IDREF	The value of a unique ID type attribute
IDREFS	Multiple whitespace-separated IDREFs of elements
NMTOKEN	An XML name token
NMTOKENS	Multiple whitespace-separated XML name tokens
NOTATION	A notation declared in the DTD

The CDATA keyword simply declares that any character data can appear, although it must adhere to the same rules as the PCDATA tag. Here are some examples of attribute declarations that use CDATA:

```
<!ATTLIST person name CDATA #REQUIRED>
<!ATTLIST person email CDATA #REQUIRED>
<!ATTLIST person company CDATA #FIXED "O'Reilly">
```

Here are two examples of enumerated datatypes where no keywords are specified. Instead, the possible values are simply listed:

```
<!ATTLIST person marital
   (single | married | divorced | widowed) #IMPLIED>
<!ATTLIST person sex (male | female) #REQUIRED>
```

The ID, IDREF, and IDREFS datatypes allow you to define attributes as IDs and ID references. An ID is simply an attribute whose value distinguishes the current element from all others in the current XML document. IDs are useful for applications to link to various sections of a document that contain an element with a uniquely tagged ID. IDREFs are attributes that reference other IDs. Consider the following XML document:

```
<?xml version="1.0" standalone="yes"?>
<!DOCTYPE sector SYSTEM sector.dtd>
<sector>
   <employee empid="e1013">Jack Russell</employee>
   <employee empid="e1014">Samuel Tessen</employee>
   <employee empid="e1015" boss="e1013">
      Terri White</employee>
   <employee empid="e1016" boss="e1014">
      Steve McAlister</employee>
</sector>
```

and its DTD:

```
<!ELEMENT sector (employee*)>
<!ELEMENT employee (#PCDATA)>
<!ATTLIST employee empid ID #REQUIRED>
<!ATTLIST employee boss IDREF #IMPLIED>
```

Here, all employees have their own identification numbers (e1013, e1014, etc.), which we define in the DTD with the ID keyword using the empid attribute. This attribute then forms an ID for each <employee> element; no two <employee> elements can have the same ID.

Attributes that only reference other elements use the IDREF datatype. In this case, the boss attribute is an IDREF because it uses only the values of other ID attributes as its values. IDs will come into play when we discuss XLink and XPointer.

The IDREFS datatype is used if you want the attribute to refer to more than one ID in its value. The IDs must be separated by whitespace. For example, adding this to the DTD:

```
<!ATTLIST employee managers IDREFS #REQUIRED>
```

allows you to legally use the XML:

```
<employee empid="e1016" boss="e1014"
          managers="e1014 e1013">
    Steve McAllister
</employee>
```

The `NMTOKEN` and `NMTOKENS` attributes declare XML name tokens. An *XML name token* is simply a legal XML name that consists of letters, digits, underscores, hyphens, and periods. It can contain a colon if it is part of a namespace. It may not contain whitespace; however, any of the permitted characters for an XML name can be the first character of an XML name token (e.g., `.profile` is a legal XML name token, but not a legal XML name). These datatypes are useful if you enumerate tokens of languages or other keyword sets that match these restrictions in the DTD.

The attribute types `ENTITY` and `ENTITIES` allow you to exploit an entity declared in the DTD. This includes unparsed entities. For example, you can link to an image as follows:

```
<!ELEMENT image EMPTY>
<!ATTLIST image src ENTITY #REQUIRED>
<!ENTITY chapterimage SYSTEM "chapimage.jpg" NDATA "jpg">
```

You can use the image as follows:

```
<image src="chapterimage">
```

The `ENTITIES` datatype allows multiple whitespace-separated references to entities, much like `IDREFS` and `NMTOKENS` allow multiple references to their datatypes.

The `NOTATION` keyword simply expects a notation that appears in the DTD with a `<!NOTATION>` declaration. Here, the `player` attribute of the `<media>` element can be either `mpeg` or `jpeg`:

```
<!NOTATION mpeg SYSTEM "mpegplay.exe">
<!NOTATION jpeg SYSTEM "netscape.exe">
<!ATTLIST media player
     NOTATION (mpeg | jpeg) #REQUIRED>
```

Note that you must enumerate each of the notations allowed in the attribute. For example, to dictate the possible values of the player attribute of the <media> element, use the following:

```
<!NOTATION mpeg SYSTEM "mpegplay.exe">
<!NOTATION jpeg SYSTEM "netscape.exe">
<!NOTATION mov SYSTEM "mplayer.exe">
<!NOTATION avi SYSTEM "mplayer.exe">
<!ATTLIST media player
      NOTATIONS (mpeg | jpeg | mov) #REQUIRED>
```

Note that according the rules of this DTD, the <media> element is not allowed to play AVI files. The NOTATION keyword is rarely used.

Finally, you can place all the ATTLIST entries for an element inside a single ATTLIST declaration, as long as you follow the rules of each datatype:

```
<!ATTLIST person
          name CDATA #REQUIRED
          number IDREF #REQUIRED
          company CDATA #FIXED "O'Reilly">
```

Included and Ignored Sections

Within a DTD, you can bundle together a group of declarations that should be ignored using the IGNORE directive:

```
<![IGNORE[
   DTD content to be ignored
]]>
```

Conversely, if you wish to ensure that certain declarations are included in your DTD, use the INCLUDE directive, which has a similar syntax:

```
<![INCLUDE[
   DTD content to be included
]]>
```

Why you would want to use either of these declarations is not obvious until you consider replacing the INCLUDE or IGNORE directives with a parameter entity reference that can be changed easily on the spot. For example, consider the following DTD:

```
<?xml version="1.0" encoding="iso-8859-1"?>
<![%book;[
   <!ELEMENT text (chapter+)>
]]>
<![%article;[
   <!ELEMENT text (section+)>
]]>
<!ELEMENT chapter (section+)>
<!ELEMENT section (p+)>
<!ELEMENT p (#PCDATA)>
```

Depending on the values of the entities `book` and `article`, the definition of the text element will be different:

- If `book` has the value `INCLUDE` and `article` has the value `IGNORE`, then the `text` element must include `chapters` (which in turn may contain `sections` that themselves include `paragraphs`).
- But if `book` has the value `IGNORE` and `article` has the value `INCLUDE`, then the `text` element must include `sections`.

When writing an XML document based on this DTD, you may write either a book or an article simply by properly defining `book` and `article` entities in the document's *internal subset.*

Internal subsets

You can place parts of your DTD declarations inside the `DOCTYPE` declaration of the XML document, as shown:

```
<!DOCTYPE boilerplate SYSTEM "generic-inc.dtd" [
   <!ENTITY corpname "Acme, Inc.">
]>
```

The region between brackets is called the DTD's internal subset. When a parser reads the DTD, the internal subset is read first, followed by the *external subset,* which is the file referenced by the `DOCTYPE` declaration.

There are restrictions on the complexity of the internal subset, as well as processing expectations that affect how you should structure it:

- Conditional sections (such as `INCLUDE` or `IGNORE`) are not permitted in an internal subset.
- Any parameter entity reference in the internal subset must expand to zero or more declarations. For example, specifying the following parameter entity reference is legal:

  ```
  %paradecl;
  ```

  as long as `%paradecl;` expands to the following:

  ```
  <!ELEMENT para CDATA>
  ```

  However, if you simply write the following in the internal subset, it is considered illegal because it does not expand to a whole declaration:

  ```
  <!ELEMENT para (%paracont;)>
  ```

Nonvalidating parsers aren't required to read the external subset and process its contents, but they are required to process any defaults and entity declarations in the internal subset. However, a parameter entity can change the meaning of those declarations in an unresolvable way. Therefore, a parser must stop processing the internal subset when it comes to the first external parameter entity reference that it does not process. If it's an internal reference, it can expand it, and if it chooses to fetch the entity, it can continue processing. If it does not process the entity's replacement, it must not process the attribute list or entity declarations in the internal subset.

Why use this? Since some entity declarations are often relevant only to a single document (for example, declarations of chapter entities or other content files), the internal subset is a good place to put them. Similarly, if a particular document needs to override or alter the DTD values it uses, you can place a new definition in the internal subset. Finally, in the event that an XML processor is nonvalidating (as we mentioned previously), the internal subset is the best place to put certain DTD-related information, such as the identification of `ID` and `IDREF` attributes, attribute defaults, and entity declarations.

The Extensible Stylesheet Language

The Extensible Stylesheet Language (XSL) is one of the most intricate specifications in the XML family. XSL can be broken into two parts: XSLT, which is used for transformations, and XSL Formatting Objects (XSL-FO). While XSLT is currently in widespread use, XSL-FO is still maturing; both, however, promise to be useful for any XML developer.

This section will provide you with a firm understanding of how XSL is meant to be used. For the very latest information on XSL, visit the home page for the W3C XSL working group at *http://www.w3.org/Style/XSL/*.

As we mentioned, XSL works by applying element-formatting rules that you define for each XML document it encounters. In reality, XSL simply transforms each XML document from one series of element types to another. For example, XSL can be used to apply HTML formatting to an XML document, which would transform it from:

```
<?xml version="1.0"?>
<OReilly:Book title="XML Comments">
 <OReilly:Chapter title="Working with XML">
  <OReilly:Image src="http://www.oreilly.com/1.gif"/>
  <OReilly:HeadA>Starting XML</OReilly:HeadA>
  <OReilly:Body>
    If you haven't used XML, then ...
  </OReilly:Body>
 </OReilly:Chapter>
</OReilly:Book>
```

to the following HTML:

```
<HTML>
  <HEAD>
   <TITLE>XML Comments</TITLE>
```

```
  </HEAD>
  <BODY>
   <H1>Working with XML</H1>
   <img src="http://www.oreilly.com/1.gif"/>
   <H2>Starting XML</H2>
   <P>If you haven't used XML, then ...</P>
  </BODY>
</HTML>
```

If you look carefully, you can see a predefined hierarchy that remains from the source content to the resulting content. To venture a guess, the <OReilly:Book> element probably maps to the <HTML>, <HEAD>, <TITLE>, and <BODY> elements in HTML. The <OReilly:Chapter> element maps to the HTML <H1> element, the <OReilly:Image> element maps to the <img> element, and so on.

This demonstrates an essential aspect of XML: each document contains a hierarchy of elements that can be organized in a tree-like fashion. (If the document uses a DTD, that hierarchy is well defined.) In the previous XML example, the <OReilly:Chapter> element is a leaf of the <OReilly:Book> element, while in the HTML document, the <BODY> and <HEAD> elements are leaves of the <HTML> element. XSL's primary purpose is to apply formatting rules to a *source tree*, rendering its results to a *result tree*, as we've just done.

However, unlike other stylesheet languages such as CSS, XSL makes it possible to transform the structure of the document. XSLT applies transformation rules to the document source and by changing the tree structure, produces a new document. It can also amalgamate several documents into one or even produce several documents starting from the same XML file.

Formatting Objects

One area of the XSL specification that is gaining steam is the idea of *formatting objects*. These objects serve as universal formatting tags that can be applied to virtually any arena, including both video and print. However, this (rather large) area of the specification is still in its infancy, so we will not discuss it further in this reference. For more information on formatting objects, see *http://www.w3.org/TR/XSL/*. The remainder of this section discusses XSL Transformations.

XSLT Stylesheet Structure

The general order for elements in an XSL stylesheet is as follows:

```
<xsl:stylesheet version="1.0"
     xmlns:xsl="http://www.w3.org/1999/XSL/Transform">
  <xsl:import/>
  <xsl:include/>
  <xsl:strip-space/>
  <xsl:preserve-space/>
  <xsl:output/>
  <xsl:key/>
  <xsl:decimal-format/>
  <xsl:namespace-alias/>
  <xsl:attribute-set>...</xsl:attribute-set>
  <xsl:variable>...</xsl:variable>
  <xsl:param>...</xsl:param>

  <xsl:template match="...">
    ...
  </xsl:template>

  <xsl:template name="...">
    ...
  </xsl:template>

</xsl:stylesheet>
```

Essentially, this ordering boils down to a few simple rules. First, all XSL stylesheets must be well-formed XML documents, and each `<XSL>` element must use the namespace specified by the `xmlns` declaration in the `<stylesheet>` element (commonly `xsl:`). Second, all XSL stylesheets must begin with the XSL root element tag, `<xsl:stylesheet>`, and close with the corresponding tag, `</xsl:stylesheet>`. Within the opening tag, the XSL namespace must be defined:

```
<xsl:stylesheet
   version="1.0"
   xmlns:xsl="http://www.w3.org/1999/XSL/Transform">
```

After the root element, you can import external stylesheets with `<xsl:import>` elements, which must always be first within the `<xsl:stylesheet>` element. Any other elements can then be used in any order and in multiple occurrences if needed.

Templates and Patterns

An XSLT stylesheet transforms an XML document by applying *templates* for a given type of node. A template element looks like this:

```
<xsl:template match="pattern">
   ...
</xsl:template>
```

where *`pattern`* selects the type of node to be processed.

For example, say you want to write a template to transform a `<para>` node (for paragraph) into HTML. This template will be applied to all `<para>` elements. The tag at the beginning of the template will be:

```
<xsl:template match="para">
```

The body of the template often contains a mix of "template instructions" and text that should appear literally in the result, although neither are required. In the previous example, we want to wrap the contents of the `<para>` element in `<p>` and `</p>` HTML tags. Thus, the template would look like this:

```
<xsl:template match="para">
   <p><xsl:apply-templates/></p>
</xsl:template>
```

The `<xsl:apply-templates/>` element recursively applies all other templates from the stylesheet against the `<para>` element (the current node) while this template is processing. Every stylesheet has at least two templates that apply by default.

The first default template processes text and attribute nodes and writes them literally in the document. The second default template is applied to elements and root nodes that have no associated namespace. In this case, no output is generated, but templates are applied recursively from the node in question.

Now that we have seen the principle of templates, we can look at a more complete example. Consider the following XML document:

```
<?xml version="1.0" encoding="iso-8859-1"?>

<!DOCTYPE text SYSTEM "example.dtd">

<chapter>
   <title>Sample text</title>
   <section title="First section">
      <para>This is the first section of the text.</para>
   </section>
   <section title="Second section">
      <para>This is the second section of the text.</para>
   </section>
</chapter>
```

To transform this into HTML, we use the following template:

```
<?xml version="1.0" encoding="iso-8859-1"?>
<xsl:stylesheet version="1.0"
   xmlns:xsl="http://www.w3.org/1999/XSL/Transform">

   <xsl:output method="html"/>

   <xsl:template match="chapter">
      <html>
         <head>
            <title><xsl:value-of select="title"/></title>
         </head>
         <body>
            <xsl:apply-templates/>
         </body>
      </html>
   </xsl:template>
```

```
    <xsl:template match="title">
       <center>
          <h1><xsl:apply-templates/></h1>
       </center>
    </xsl:template>

    <xsl:template match="section">
       <h3><xsl:value-of select="@title"/></h3>
       <xsl:apply-templates/>
    </xsl:template>

    <xsl:template match="para">
       <p><xsl:apply-templates/></p>
    </xsl:template>

</xsl:stylesheet>
```

Let's look at how this stylesheet works. As processing begins, the current node is the document root (not to be confused with the `<chapter>` element, which is its only descendant), designated as `/` (like the root directory in a Unix filesystem). The XSLT processor searches the stylesheet for a template with a matching pattern in any children of the root. Only the first template matches (`<xsl:template match="chapter">`). The first template is then applied to the `<chapter>` node, which becomes the current node.

The transformation then takes place: the `<html>`, `<head>`, `<title>`, and `<body>` elements are simply copied into the document because they are not XSL instructions. Between the tags `<head>` and `</head>`, the `<xsl:value-of select="title"/>` element copies the contents of the `<title>` element into the document. Finally, the `<xsl:apply-templates/>` element tells the XSL processor to apply the templates recursively and insert the result between the `<body>` and `</body>` tags.

This time through, the title and section templates are applied because their patterns match. The title template inserts the contents of the `<title>` element between the HTML `<center>` and `<h1>` tags, thus displaying the document title. The section template works by using the `<xsl:value-of select="@title">` element to recopy the contents of the current element's `title` attribute into the document produced. We can indicate in a pattern that we want to copy the value of an attribute by placing the at symbol (`@`) in front of its name.

The process continues recursively to produce the following HTML document:

```
<html>
   <head>
      <title>Sample text</title>
   </head>
   <body>
      <center>
         <h1>Sample text</h1>
      </center>
      <h3>First section</h3>
      <p>This is the first section of the text.</p>
      <h3>Second section</h3>
      <p>This is the second section of the text.</p>
   </body>
</html>
```

As you will see later, patterns are XPath expressions for locating nodes in an XML document. This example includes very basic patterns, and we have only scratched the surface of what can be done with templates. More information will be found in the section "XPath."

In addition, the `<xsl:template>` element has a `mode` attribute that can be used for conditional processing. An `<xsl:template match="`*`pattern`*`" mode="`*`mode`*`">` template is tested only when it is called by an `<xsl:apply-templates mode="`*`mode`*`">` element that matches its mode. This functionality can be used to change the processing applied to a node dynamically.

Parameters and Variables

To finish up with templates, we should discuss the `name` attribute. These templates are similar to functions and can be called explicitly with the `<xsl:call-template name="`*`name`*`"/>` element, where *`name`* matches the name of the template you want to invoke. When you call a template, you can pass it parameters. Let's assume we wrote a template to add a footer containing the date the document was last updated. We could call the template, passing it the date of the last update this way:

```
<xsl:call-template name="footer">
<xsl:with-param name="date" select="@lastupdate"/>
</xsl:call-template>
```

The `call-template` declares and uses the parameter this way:

```
<xsl:template name="footer">
   <xsl:param name="date">today</xsl:param>
   <hr/>
   <xsl:text>Last update: </xsl:text>
   <xsl:value-of select="$date"/>
</xsl:template>
```

The parameter is declared within the template with the `<xsl:param name="date">` element whose content (`today`) provides a default value. We can use this parameter inside the template by placing a dollar sign ($) in front of the name.

We can also declare variables using the `<xsl:variable name="`*`name`*`">` element, where the content of the element gives the variable its value. The variables are used like parameters by placing a dollar sign ($) in front of their names. Note that even though they are called variables, their values are constant and cannot be changed. A variable's visibility also depends on where it is declared. A variable that is declared directly as a child element of `<xsl:stylesheet>` can be used throughout the stylesheet as a global variable. Conversely, when a variable is declared in the body of the template, it is visible only within that same template.

Stylesheet Import and Rules of Precedence

Stylesheets may be imported using the `<xsl:import href="`*`uri`*`">` element, where the `href` attribute indicates the path of the stylesheet to be imported. Note that an `<xsl:import>` statement must be a direct child of the `<xsl:stylesheet>` element.

Imported stylesheet templates have lower precedence than templates contained in the file into which they are incorporated. This means that if two templates compete for the processing of an element, the template of the original file takes precedence over the template of the imported file. Thus, imported templates can be overridden by redefining them in the original stylesheet.

The rules of precedence can be changed in two ways:

- The `<xsl:apply-imports/>` element can be used to give imported templates precedence in the body of a template.
- The `priority="`*`level`*`"` attribute can be given in the opening `<xsl:template>` tag. Therefore, the level of precedence defined for the template is a real number. The larger the number, the more precedence the template has. A value of +1 ensures that the template has precedence over other templates for which no precedence has been defined (0 is the default). A value of –1 guarantees that any other unprioritized template has precedence. Priority values overrule import precedence.

Stylesheets can also be included in an XSL file with the `<xsl:include href="`*`uri`*`"/>` element. The precedence of an included template is the same as that of the calling stylesheet templates.

Loops and Tests

To process an entire list of elements at the same time, use the `<xsl:for-each>` loop. For example, the following template adds a table of contents to our example:

```
<xsl:template name="toc">
<xsl:for-each select="section">
<xsl:value-of select="@title"/>
<br/>
</xsl:for-each>
</xsl:template>
```

The body of this `<xsl:for-each>` loop processes all the `<section>` elements that are children of the current node. Within the loop, we output the value of each section's `title` attribute, followed by a line break.

XSL also defines elements that can be used for tests:

`<xsl:if test="`*`expression`*`">`
: The body of this element is executed only if the test expression is true.

`<xsl:choose>`
: This element allows for several possible conditions. It is comparable to `switch` in the C and Java languages. The `<xsl:choose>` element is illustrated as follows:

```
<xsl:choose>
   <xsl:when test="case-1">
      <!-- executed in case 1 -->
   </xsl:when>
   <xsl:when test="case-2">
      <!-- executed in case 2 -->
   </xsl:when>

   <xsl:otherwise>
      <!-- executed by default -->
   </xsl:otherwise>
</xsl:choose>
```

The body of the first `<xsl:when>` element whose test expression is true will be executed. The XSL processor then moves on to the instructions following the closing `</xsl:choose>` element tag, skipping the remaining tests. The `<xsl:otherwise>` element is optional; its body is executed only if none of the preceding elements were executed.

Numbering Elements

XSL provides a simple method for numbering elements with the `<xsl:number>` element. Let's assume we want to number the sections and paragraphs in a document. We can do this by adding the following code before displaying the section titles and the content of the paragraphs:

```
<xsl:number count="sect|para"
   level="multiple" format="1.1"/>
<xsl:text>- </xsl:text>
```

The result is:

```
1 - First section
1.1 - This is the first section of text.
2 - Second section
2.1 - This is the second section of text.
```

The `count` attribute decides which elements should be numbered. Elements must be separated by a `|`. The `level` attribute specifies the level of numbering and may take one of three string values: `single`, `multiple`, or `any`. `single` tells the processor to number only one level. In this case, paragraph numbers will not indicate the section number. `multiple` numbers several levels, meaning that the first part of the paragraph number is the section number in our previous example. `any` tells the processor to add numbering without regard to level. Here, the numbers of the sections and paragraphs are consecutive.

The format attribute indicates the style of numbering. Letters or numbers may be used, with a separator in between. The letters may be `A` or `a` (for alphabetical numbering in upper- or lowercase), `I` or `i` (for numbering in upper- or lowercase Roman numerals), or `1` (for numbering in Arabic numerals). For example, to number sections with Roman numerals and paragraphs with lowercase letters, use this format attribute:

```
format="I.a"
```

Output Method

An XSLT processor can be instructed to produce a specific type of output with the `<xsl:output/>` element. For example, `<xsl:output method="html"/>` causes the processor to execute certain transformations needed for the resulting document to be valid HTML. Specifically, it transforms empty tags. For example, the XML `<hr/>` tag is converted to the HTML `<hr>` tag (for horizontal rules) without a closing slash.

It is also possible to indicate an XML output method (`method="xml"`), where the XSLT processor adds the standard XML header (`<?xml version="1.0"?>`). It may seem strange to produce an XML document from another XML document, yet it is often helpful to convert a document from one DTD to a valid document for another DTD. Thus, XSLT is also a language for inter-DTD conversions.

Finally, you can specify a text output method (`method="text"`) to produce pure text. XSLT has built-in outputs for XML, HTML, and text, but some processors may support other output methods (sometimes identified by URLs).

We should point out that when you choose the HTML or XML output method, the processor may remove or rearrange whitespace in blocks of text (spaces, tabs, and carriage returns). However, there are several solutions for preserving whitespace. The first is to indicate the list of elements to be preserved in the `<xsl:preserve-space elements="`*`list`*`">` element. The second is to add the `indent="no"` attribute to the `<xsl:output>` element to indicate that you do not want the resulting document to be indented. We should point out, however, that spaces are no longer preserved in `<xsl:text>` elements where content is written as-is in the resulting document. No indenting is produced for the text output method.

XSLT Elements

The following list is an enumeration of XSLT elements.

<xsl:apply-imports>

```
<xsl:apply-imports/>
```

This styles the current node and each of its children using the imported stylesheet rules, ignoring those in the stylesheet that performed the import. Note that the rules don't apply to the current node's siblings or ancestors.

<xsl:apply-templates>

```
<xsl:apply-templates
   [select="node-set-expression"]
   [mode="mode"]/>
```

This specifies that the immediate children (default) or the selected nodes of the source element should be processed further. For example:

```
<xsl:template match="section">
     <B><xsl:apply-templates/><B>
</xsl:template>
```

This example processes the children of the selected `<section>` element after applying a bold tag. The optional `select` attribute determines which nodes should be processed:

```
<xsl:template match="section">
   <HR>
   <xsl:apply-templates
      select="paragraph (@indent)//sidebar"/>
   <HR>
   <xsl:apply-templates
      select="paragraph (@indent)/quote"/>
   <HR>
</xsl:template>
```

This example processes only specific children of the selected `<section>` element. In this case, the first target is a `<sidebar>` element that is a descendant of a `<paragraph>` element that has defined an `indent` attribute. The second target is a `<quote>` element that is the direct child of a `<paragraph>` element that has defined an `indent` attribute. The optional `mode` attribute causes only templates with a matching `mode` to be applied.

<xsl:attribute>

```
<xsl:attribute name="name"
   [namespace="namespace"]>
   ...
</xsl:attribute>
```

This adds an attribute with the given name to an element in the result tree. Only one attribute with a particular name can be added to a specific element. The contents of the `<xsl:attribute>` element form the value of the attribute:

```
<xsl:element name="book">
<xsl:attribute name="title">Moby Dick</xsl:attribute>
<xsl:text>This is about a whale</xsl:text>
</xsl:element>
```

This creates the following element in the result tree:

```
<book title="Moby Dick">This is about a whale</book>
```

The optional `namespace` attribute specifies a namespace for the new attribute.

<xsl:attribute-set>

```
<xsl:attribute-set
   name="name"
   [use-attribute-sets="list"]/>
```

This allows the naming of a collection of attributes that can be applied to elements.

The following example creates an attribute set for images and applies them with a template:

```
<xsl:attribute-set name="image">
   <xsl:attribute name="border">0</xsl:attribute>
   <xsl:attribute name="width">120</xsl:attribute>
   <xsl:attribute name="height">60</xsl:attribute>
</xsl:attribute-set>
```

```
<xsl:template match="image">
   <img src="{@url}" xsl:use-attribute-sets="image"/>
</xsl:template>
```

The use-attribute-sets option allows you to include a list of other attribute sets in the one being defined.

<xsl:call-template>

```
<xsl:call-template
   name="name">
   ...
</xsl:call-template>
```

This function invokes a template by its name. It is possible to specify parameters in the body of this element. The following example calls the template image while passing the parameters width and height:

```
<xsl:call-template name="image">
   <xsl:with-param name="width">120</xsl:with-param>
   <xsl:with-param name="height">60</xsl:with-param>
</xsl:call-template>
```

<xsl:choose>

```
<xsl:choose>
   ...
</xsl:choose>
```

The <xsl:choose> element, in conjunction with the elements <xsl:when> and <xsl:otherwise>, offers the ability to perform multiple condition tests. For example:

```
<xsl:template match="chapter/title">
   <xsl:choose>
      <xsl:when test="[position()=1]">
          Start Here:
      </xsl:when>
      <xsl:otherwise>
          Then Read:
       </xsl:otherwise>
   </xsl:choose>
   <xsl:apply-templates/>
</xsl:template>
```

This example matches against each of the qualifying `<title>` elements, but it must test each `<title>` element to determine how to format it. Here, formatting depends on whether the element is first. The string `Start Here:` is applied before the first `<title>` element, and the string `Then Read:` is placed before the others.

<xsl:comment>

```
<xsl:comment>
   ...
</xsl:comment>
```

This inserts a comment into the XML document. For example:

```
<xsl:comment>English material below</xsl:comment>
```

is translated into a comment in the XML result tree when it is processed:

```
<!-- English material below -->
```

<xsl:copy>

```
<xsl:copy
   [use-attribute-sets="list"]>
   ...
</xsl:copy>
```

This element copies the current node from the source document into the output document. This copies the node itself, as well as any namespace nodes the node possesses. However, it does not copy the node's content or attributes.

The `use-attribute-sets` attribute contains a whitespace-separated list with names of `<xsl:attribute-set>` elements. These attribute sets are merged, and all attributes in the merged set are added to the copied element. The `use-attribute-sets` attribute can only be used when the node copied is an element node.

<xsl:copy-of>

```
<xsl:copy-of
  select="expression"/>
```

The `<xsl:copy-of>` instruction inserts the result tree fragment identified by the `select` attribute into the output document. This copies not only the specific node or nodes identified by the expression, but also all those nodes' children, attributes, namespaces, and descendants. (This is how it differs from `xsl:copy`.) If the expression selects something other than a node set or a result tree fragment (e.g., a number), then the expression is converted to its string value, and the string is output.

<xsl:decimal-format>

```
<xsl:decimal-format
  [name ="name"]
  [decimal-separator = "char"]
  [grouping-separator = "char"]
  [infinity = "string"]
  [minus-sign = "char"]
  [NaN = "string"]
  [percent = "char"]
  [per-mille = "char"]
  [zero-digit = "char"]
  [digit = "char"]
  [pattern-separator = "char"]/>
```

The `<xsl:decimal-format>` element defines a pattern by which the XPath `format-number()` function can convert floating-point numbers into text strings. The attributes are specified as follows:

`name`
: The string by which the `format-number()` function identifies which `<xsl:decimal-format>` element to use. If this attribute is omitted, then the element establishes the default decimal format used by the `format-number()` function.

`decimal-separator`
: The character that separates the integer part from the fractional part in a floating-point number. This is a period (decimal point) in English and a comma in French. It may be something else again in other languages.

`grouping-separator`
: The character that separates groups of digits (e.g., the comma that separates every three digits in English).

`infinity`
: The string that represents IEEE 754 infinity; Infinity by default.

`minus-sign`
: The character prefixed to negative numbers; a hyphen by default.

`NaN`
: The string that represents IEEE 754 Not a Number; NaN by default.

`percent`
: The character that represents a percent; % by default.

`per-mille`
: The character that represents a per mille; #x2030 by default.

`zero-digit`
: The character that represents zero in a format pattern; 0 by default.

`digit`
: The character that represents a digit in a format pattern; # by default.

`pattern-separator`
: The character that separates positive and negative subpatterns in a format pattern; a semicolon (;) by default.

<xsl:element>

```
<xsl:element
   name="name"
   [namespace="URI"]
   [use-attribute-sets="list"]>
   ...
</xsl:element>
```

This inserts the element <name> into the result document. For example:

```
<xsl:element name="book">
   <xsl:element name="chapter">
      <xsl:text>The Opening of Pandora's Box</xsl:text>
   </xsl:element>
</xsl:element>
```

This creates the following in the result tree:

```
<book>
   <chapter>The Opening of Pandora's Box</chapter>
</book>
```

Elements without explicit namespaces use the default namespace of their current context. Also, you can create a namespace for the element yourself:

```
<xsl:element name="OReilly:Book"
   namespace="http://www.oreilly.com">
```

This employs the namespace associated with the URI *http://www.oreilly.com* with the element. If no namespaces are associated with the URI, it becomes the default namespace.

The `use-attribute-sets` attribute contains a whitespace-separated list with names of `<xsl:attribute-set>` elements. These attribute sets are merged, and all attributes in the merged set are added to the element.

<xsl:fallback>

```
<xsl:fallback> ... </xsl:fallback>
```

This element is used in conjunction with *extension elements* that aren't a part of XSLT 1.0. `<xsl:fallback>` defines a template to be invoked if the enclosing element is undefined. It's possible to test the availability of an element with `element-available()`.

<xsl:for-each>

```
<xsl:for-each select="node-set-expression"/>
```

The `<xsl:for-each>` directive allows you to select any number of nodes in an XML document that match the same expression given by `select`. For example, consider the following XML document:

```
<book>
   <chapter>
      <title>A Mystery Unfolds</title>
      <paragraph>
      It was a dark and stormy night...
      </paragraph>
   </chapter>
   <chapter>
      <title>A Sudden Visit</title>
      <paragraph>
      Marcus found himself sleeping...
      </paragraph>
   </chapter>
</book>
```

Note there are two `<chapter>` siblings in the document. Let's assume we want to provide an HTML numbered list for each `<title>` element that is the direct child of a `<chapter>` element, which in turn has a `<book>` element as a parent. The following template performs the task:

```
<xsl:template match="book>
   <ol>
   <xsl:for-each select="chapter">
      <li><xsl:process select="title"></li>
   </xsl:for-each>
   </ol>
</xsl:template>
```

After formatting, here is what the result looks like:

```
<ol>
<li>A Mystery Unfolds</li>
<li>A Sudden Visit</li>
</ol>
```

The XSLT processor processes a `<title>` element in each `<chapter>` element that is the child of a `<book>` element. The result is a numbered list of chapters that could be used for a table of contents.

<xsl:if>

```
<xsl:if
  test="expression">
  ...
</xsl:if>
```

You can use the `<xsl:if>` conditional to select a specific element while inside a template. The `<xsl:if>` element uses the `test` attribute to determine whether to include the contents of an element. The `test` attribute takes an expression that tests for a specific element or attribute. For example:

```
<xsl:template match="chapter/title">
   <xsl:apply-templates/>
   <xsl:if test="not([last()])">, </xsl:if>
</xsl:template>
```

This template matches each qualifying `<title>` element but inserts commas only after those that are not the last `<title>` element. The result is a standard comma-separated list.

<xsl:import>

```
<xsl:import href="address"/>
```

This specifies the URI of an XSL stylesheet whose rules should be imported into this stylesheet. The `import` statement must occur before any other elements in the stylesheet. If a conflict arises between matching rules, rules in the XSL stylesheet performing the import take precedence over rules in the imported stylesheet. In addition, if more than one stylesheet is imported into this document, the most recently imported stylesheet takes precedence over stylesheets imported before it:

```
<xsl:import href="webpage.xsl"/>
```

This example imports the stylesheet found in the *webpage.xsl* file.

<xsl:include>

```
<xsl:include href="address"/>
```

This specifies the name of an XSL stylesheet that is to be included in the document. The `include` processing will replace the `<xsl:include>` statement with the contents of the file. Because the included document has been inserted in the referring stylesheet, any included rules have the same preference as those in the referring stylesheet (compare to `<xsl:import>`):

```
<xsl:include href="chapterFormats.xsl"/>
```

<xsl:key>

```
<xsl:key name="name"
   match="pattern"
   use="expression"/>
```

Keys are comparable to identifiers in XML. This element is used in `<xsl:stylesheet>` to create a reference to elements specified by the pattern and expression values. For example:

```
<xsl:key name="chap" match="chapter" use="@title"/>
```

This element creates a key named `chap` to identify chapters by title. You can then reference a chapter with an XPath function such as:

```
key("chap", "The XSL Language")
```

<xsl:message>

```
<xsl:message [terminate="yes|no"]>
   ...
</xsl:message>
```

The `<xsl:message>` instruction asks the XSLT processor to send a message to the user or calling program. Exactly what it does with those messages depends on the processor. One common use of `<xsl:message>` is to print debugging information.

If the `terminate` attribute is present and has the value `yes`, then the XSLT processor should halt after the message has been delivered and acted on.

<xsl:namespace-alias>

```
<xsl:namespace-alias
   stylesheet-prefix="prefix1"
   result-prefix="prefix2"/>
```

The `<xsl:namespace-alias>` element declares that one namespace URI (*`prefix1`*) in the stylesheet should be replaced by a different namespace URI (*`prefix2`*) in the result tree. Either attribute value can be set to `#default` to indicate that the non-prefixed default namespace is to be used.

<xsl:number>

```
<xsl:number
   [value = "expression"]
   [count = "pattern"]
   [from = "pattern"]
   [level = "single|multiple|any"]
   [format = "letter/digit"]
   [lang = "langcode"]
   [letter-value = "alphabetic|traditional"]
   [grouping-separator = "char"]
   [grouping-size = "number"] />
```

This element inserts a formatted integer into the result tree. The value of this number can be determined by the attributes or generated by the XSLT processor. The attributes are described as follows:

`value`
: This attribute contains an XPath expression returning the number to be formatted. If necessary, the number is rounded to the nearest integer. Most commonly, the `value` attribute is omitted, in which case the number is calculated from the position of the current node in the source document. The position is calculated as specified by the `level`, `count`, and `from` attributes.

`count`
: This attribute contains a pattern that specifies which nodes should be counted at those levels. The default is to count all nodes of the same node type (element, text, attribute, etc.) and name as the current node.

`from`
: This attribute contains a pattern identifying the node from which counting starts; that is, it says which node is number 1.

`level`
: This attribute can be set to `single` (all preceding siblings of the ancestor of the current node that match the `count`

pattern), `multiple` (for nested counting of each type of ancestor of the current node that match the `count` pattern), or `any` (count all nodes in the document that match the `count` pattern and precede the current node). The default is `single`.

`format`
: This attribute determines how the list will be numbered. Format tokens include:

- 1, 2, 3, 4, 5, 6
- 01, 02, 03, 04, 05, 06, 07, 08, 09, 10, 11, 12
- A, B, C, D . . . Z, AA, AB, AC . . .
- a, b, c, d . . . z, aa, ab, ac . . .
- i, ii, iii, iv, v, vi, vii, viii, ix, x, xi . . .
- I, II, III, IV, V, VI, VII, VIII, IX, X, XI, XII . . .

You can change the starting point as well. For instance, setting the format token to 5 would create the sequence 5, 6, 7, 8, 9.

`lang`
: This contains the RFC 1766 language code describing the language in which the number should be formatted (e.g., `en` or `fr`).

`letter-value`
: The default is `traditional`. However, you can set this to `alphabetic` to indicate that a format of I should start the sequence I, J, K, L, M, N rather than I, II, III, IV, V, VI.

`grouping-separator`
: This specifies the character that separates groups of digits. For instance, in English this is customarily the comma that separates every three digits, as in 2,987,667,342. In French a space is used instead so this number would be written as 2 987 667 342.

`grouping-size`
: This specifies the number of digits in each group. In most languages, including English, digits are divided into groups of three. However, a few languages use groups of four instead.

<xsl:otherwise>

```
<xsl:otherwise>...</xsl:otherwise>
```

This attribute specifies the default case in an `<xsl:choose>` element. See the "<xsl:choose>" entry earlier in this reference section.

<xsl:output>

```
<xsl:output
   [method = "xml|html|text"]
   [version = "nmtoken"]
   [encoding = "encoding_name"]
   [omit-xml-declaration = "yes|no"]
   [standalone = "yes|no"]
   [doctype-public = "public_id"]
   [doctype-system = "system_id"]
   [cdata-section-elements = "element1 element2 ..."]
   [indent = "yes|no"]
   [media-type = "string"]/>
```

The `<xsl:output>` element helps determine the exact formatting of the XML document produced when the result tree is stored in a file, written onto a stream, or otherwise serialized into a sequence of bytes. It has no effect on the production of the result tree itself. The following attributes are defined:

`method`
: The default method is `xml`, which simply implies that the serialized output document will be a well-formed parsed entity or XML document. If `method` is set to `html`, or if the method attribute is not present and the root element of the output tree is `<html>`, then empty element tags such as `<br/>` are converted to `<br>` when output, and a variety of other changes are to attempt to generate HTML that is

more compatible with existing browsers. The text method only outputs the contents of the text nodes in the output tree. It strips all markup. XSLT processors are also allowed to recognize and support other values such as TeX or RTF.

version
: This contains a name token that identifies the version of the output method. In practice, this has no effect on the output.

encoding
: This contains the name of the encoding the outputter should use, such as ISO-8859-1 or UTF-16.

omit-xml-declaration
: If this has the value yes, then no XML declaration is included. If it has the value no or is not present, then an XML declaration is included.

standalone
: This sets the value of the standalone attribute in the XML declaration. Like that attribute, it must have the value yes or no.

doctype-public
: This specifies the public identifier used in the document type declaration.

doctype-system
: This specifies the system identifier used in the document type declaration.

cdata-section-elements
: This is a whitespace-separated list of the qualified element names in the result tree whose contents should be emitted using a CDATA section rather than a character reference.

indent
: If this has the value yes, the processor is allowed (but not required) to insert extra whitespace to attempt to "pretty-print" the output tree. The default is no.

media-type
: This specifies the MIME media type of the output, such as `text/html` or `text/xml`.

<xsl:param>

```
<xsl:param
   name="name"
   [select="expression"]>
   ...
</xsl:param>
```

An `<xsl:param>` element binds its contents to the specified name, which can be called from and included in a template. As a top-level element, `<xsl:param>` provides a default value used if the named parameter is not supplied when a stylesheet is called. An `<xsl:param>` element may also appear inside an `<xsl:template>` element to receive the values of the parameters passed in with `<xsl:with-param>`, and to provide a default value good only inside that template for the case where a proper `<xsl:with-param>` element is not used. If the `select` attribute is included, its value becomes the default value of the parameter, in which case the value of the content should be empty.

<xsl:preserve-space>

```
<xsl:preserve-space
  elements="element1 element2 ..."/>
```

This declares one or more XML elements in which all whitespace located between the opening and closing tags is preserved; hence, the XML processor will not remove it. By default, whitespace is not removed from elements; `<xsl:preserve-space>` can override any elements declared in the `<xsl:strip-space>` directive:

```
<xsl:preserve-space elements="title"/>
```

<xsl:processing-instruction>

```
<xsl:processing-instruction
   name="name">
   ...
<xsl:processing-instruction>
```

The `<xsl:processing-instruction>` element inserts a processing instruction into the result tree. This element cannot be used to generate an XML declaration; use `<xsl:output>` for that. The `name` attribute specifies the target of the processing instruction.

<xsl:sort>

```
<xsl:sort
   select = "expression"
   [data-type = "text|number"]
   [lang = "langcode"]
   [order = "ascending|descending"]
   [case-order = "upper-first|lower-first"]/>
```

The `<xsl:sort>` instruction appears as a child of either `<xsl:apply-templates>` or `<xsl:for-each>`. It changes the order of the context node list from document order to some other order, such as alphabetic. Multiple-key sorts (for example, sort by last name, then by first name, then by middle name) can be performed with multiple `<xsl:sort>` elements in descending order of importance of the keys. The following attributes are defined:

`select`
: This contains the key to sort by.

`data-type`
: By default, sorting is purely alphabetic. However, alphabetic sorting leads to strange results with numbers. For instance, 10, 100, and 1000 all sort before 2, 3, and 4. You can specify numeric sorting by setting the `data-type` attribute to `number`.

`lang`
: Sorting is language dependent. The language can be adjusted by setting the `lang` attribute to an RFC 1766 language code. The default language is system dependent.

`order`
: This specifies the order by which strings are sorted. The value can be either `descending` or `ascending`. The default is `ascending`.

`case-order`
: The `case-order` attribute can be set to `upper-first` or `lower-first` to specify whether uppercase letters sort before lowercase letters or vice versa. The default depends on the language.

<xsl:strip-space>

```
<xsl:strip-space
   elements="element1 element2 ..."/>
```

This declares an XML element or list of elements in which all whitespace located between the opening and closing tags is insignificant and should be removed by the XSL processor:

```
<xsl:strip-space elements="title"/>
```

Note that this is not necessarily the same as the `xml:space="default"` attribute, which allows the XSL processor more freedom to decide how to handle whitespace.

<xsl:stylesheet>

```
<xsl:stylesheet
   version = "number"
   xmlns:xsl="http://www.w3.org/1999/XSL/Transform"
   [id = "id"]
   [extension-element-prefixes = "prefix1 prefix2..."]
   [exclude-result-prefixes = "prefixa prefixb..."]>
   ...
</xsl:stylesheet>
```

The <xsl:stylesheet> element is the root element for XSLT stylesheets. The contents of this element must first contain any <xsl:import> elements, followed by any other top-level elements in any order. <xsl:stylesheet> uses the following attributes:

`version`
: The version number of XSLT used by the stylesheet.

`xmlns:xsl`
: This attribute contains a standard namespace declaration that maps the prefix `xsl` to the namespace URI *http://www.w3.org/1999/XSL/Transform*. The prefix can be changed if necessary. This attribute is technically optional, but de facto required.

`id`
: Any XML name that's unique within the stylesheet and is of type `ID`.

`extension-element-prefixes`
: A whitespace-separated list of namespace prefixes used by extension elements in this document.

`exclude-result-prefixes`
: A whitespace-separated list of namespace prefixes whose declarations should not be copied into the output document. If a namespace is needed in the output, it will be copied regardless.

<xsl:template>

```
<xsl:template
   [match = "pattern"]
   [priority = "number"]
   [name = "name"]
   [mode = "mode"]>
   ...
</xsl:template>
```

The <xsl:template> top-level element is the key to all of XSLT. The `match` attribute contains a pattern against which nodes are compared as they're processed. If the pattern is the best match for a node, then the contents are instantiated and inserted into the output tree. This element uses the following attributes:

`match`
: A pattern against which nodes can be compared. This pattern is a location path that uses the abbreviated XPath syntax. Only the child and attribute axes may be used. The `//` separator may also be used.

`priority`
: A number. In the event that more than one template matches a given node, the one that most specifically matches the node is chosen. If several templates match a node with the same level of specificity, then the template with the highest value of the `priority` attribute is instantiated. If several matching templates have equal priorities, then the last one in the stylesheet is chosen (the processor may also throw an error in this situation).

`name`
: A name by which this template can be invoked from an `<xsl:call-template>` element rather than by node matching.

`mode`
: The template's mode. If the `<xsl:template>` element has a mode, then this template is only matched when the `mode` attribute of the calling instruction matches the value of this `mode` attribute.

<xsl:text>

```
<xsl:text>
   [disable-output-escaping="yes|no"]>
   ...
</xsl:text>
```

This inserts text verbatim into the document. For example:

```
<xsl:text>The price is $20.00.</xsl:text>
```

is inserted into the XML document as:

```
The price is $20.00.
```

XML special characters (such as & and <) included in the content of this element are escaped (i.e., replaced by character entities) in the output by default. The attribute `disable-output-escaping` can be set to `yes` to disable this behavior.

<xsl:value-of>

```
<xsl:value-of select="expression">
  [disable-output-escaping="yes|no"]/>
```

This extracts a specific value from a source tree. The `select` attribute is a single pattern-matching expression that resolves to the value of a string, an element, or an attribute:

```
<xsl:template match="index">
   This index is <xsl:value-of select="@(type)">
   <xsl:apply-templates/>
</xsl:template>
```

The `select` attribute extracts the value of an element or attribute in the source tree and prints it verbatim in the result tree. XML special characters (such as & and <) included in the content of this element are escaped (i.e., replaced by character entities) in the output by default. The attribute `disable-output-escaping` can be set to `yes` to disable this behavior.

<xsl:variable>

```
<xsl:variable
  name="name"
  [select="expression"]>
  ...
</xsl:variable>
```

The top-level `<xsl:variable>` element binds a name to a value of any type (string, number, node set, etc.). The value can then be dereferenced elsewhere in the stylesheet using the form `$name` in attribute value templates. Once a variable name has been assigned a value, it cannot change. The `select` attribute is an optional expression that sets the value of the variable. If `<xsl:variable>` has a `select` attribute, then it must be an empty element.

<xsl:when>

```
<xsl:when
   test="expression">
   ...
</xsl:when>
```

This is a conditional for testing in an `<xsl:choose>` element. See the "<xsl:choose>" entry earlier in this reference section.

<xsl:with-param>

```
<xsl:with-param
   name="name"
   [select="expression"]>
   ...
</xsl:with-param>
```

The `<xsl:with-param>` element passes a named parameter to a template that expects it. It can be a child either of `<xsl:apply-templates>` or `<xsl:call-template>`. The parameter is received in the `<xsl:template>` by an `<xsl:param>` element with the same name. If a template expects to receive a particular parameter and doesn't get it, then it can take the default from the value of the `<xsl:param>` element instead.

XPath

XPath is a recommendation of the World Wide Web Consortium (W3C) for locating nodes in an XML document tree. XPath is not designed to be used alone but in conjunction with other tools, such as XSLT or XPointer. These tools use XPath intensively and extend it for their own needs through new functions and new basic types.

XPath provides a syntax for locating a node in an XML document. It takes its inspiration from the syntax used to denote paths in filesystems such as Unix. This node, often called the *context node*, depends on the context of the XPath expression. For example, the context of an XSLT expression found in an `<xsl:template match="para">` template will be the selected `<para>` element (recall that XSLT templates use XPath expressions). This node can be compared to a Unix shell's current directory.

Given our earlier XML examples, it is possible to write the following expressions:

`chapter`
: Selects the `<chapter>` element descendants of the context node

`chapter/para`
: Selects the `<para>` element descendants of the `<chapter>` element children of the context node

`../chapter`
: Selects the `<chapter>` element descendants of the parent of the context node

`./chapter`
: Selects the `<chapter>` element descendants of the context node

`*`
: Selects all element children of the context node

`*/para`
: Selects the `<para>` grandchildren of the context node

`.//para`
: Selects the `<para>` element descendants (children, children of children, etc.) of the context node

`/para`
: Selects the `<para>` element children of the document root element

In addition, XPath recognizes the at symbol (@) for selecting an attribute instead of an element. Thus the following expressions can be used to select an attribute:

`para/@id`
: Selects the `id` attribute of the `<para>` element descendants of the context node

`@*`
: Selects all the attributes in the context node

Paths can be combined using the | operator. For example, `intro | chapter` selects the `<intro>` and `<chapter>` elements of the children of the context node.

Certain functions can also be included in the path. The functions must return a node or set of nodes. The functions available are:

Function	Selection
`node( )`	Any node (of any type)
`text( )`	Text node
`comment( )`	Comment node
`processing-instruction( )`	Processing-instruction node
`id(`*`id`*`)`	Node whose unique identifier is *`id`*

The `id()` function is especially helpful for locating a node by its unique identifier (recall that identifiers are attributes defined by the DTD). For example, we can write the expression `id("xml-ref")/title` to select the `<title>` element whose parent has the `xml-ref` identifier.

The preceding examples show that the analogy with file paths is rather limited. However, this syntax for writing an XPath expression is a simplification of the more complete XPath syntax where an axis precedes each step in the path.

Axes

Axes indicate the direction taken by the path. In the previous examples, the syntactic qualifiers such as `/` for root, `..` for parent, and `//` for descendant, are abbreviations that indicate the axis of the node search. These are some of the simple axes on which to search for a node.

XPath defines other search axes that are indicated by a prefix separated from the rest of the XPath expression (called *location-steps*) by a double colon. For example, to indicate that we require a `para` node to be the parent of the context node in the document, we could write the expression `preceding::para`. XPath defines 13 axes:

Axis	Selection
`self`	The context node itself (abbreviated as `.`)
`child`	The children of the context node (by default)
`descendant`	The descendants of the context node; a descendant is a child, or a child of a child, and so on
`descendant-or-self`	Same as the descendant, but also contains the context node (abbreviated as `//`)
`parent`	The parent of the context node (abbreviated as `..`)
`ancestor`	The ancestors of the context node
`ancestor-or-self`	The same nodes as the ancestor, plus the context node
`following-sibling`	Siblings (having the same parent as the context node) in the same document that are after the context node
`preceding-sibling`	Siblings in the same document that are before the context node
`following`	All nodes in the same document that are after the context node
`preceding`	All nodes in the same document that are before the context node

Axis	Selection
`attribute`	The attributes of the context node (abbreviated as `@`)
`namespace`	The namespace nodes of the context node

It is possible to write the following expressions:

`ancestor::chapter`
: Selects the `<chapter>` elements that are ancestors of the context node

`following-sibling::para/@title`
: Selects the `title` attributes of `<para>` elements in siblings of the context node that follow it in document order

`id('xpath')/following::chapter/node()`
: Selects all the nodes in the `<chapter>` element following the element with the `xpath` identifier in document order

The result of an XPath expression is a node-set. It may be helpful to filter a node-set with predicates.

Predicates

A predicate is an expression in square brackets that filters a node-set. For example, we could write the following expressions:

`//chapter[1]`
: Selects the first `<chapter>` element in the document

`//chapter[@title='XPath']`
: Selects the `<chapter>` element in the document where the value of the `title` attribute is the string `XPath`

`//chapter[section]`
: Selects the `<chapter>` elements in the document with a `<section>` child

`<para[last()]>`
: Selects the last `<para>` element child of the context node

Note that a path in a predicate does not change the path preceding the predicate, but only filters it. Thus, the following expression:

```
/book/chapter[conclusion]
```

selects a `<chapter>` element that is a child of the `<book>` element at the root of the document with a descendant of type `conclusion`, but not a `<conclusion>` element itself.

There may be more than one predicate in an expression. The following expression:

```
/book/chapter[1]/section[2]
```

selects the second section of the first chapter. In addition, the order of the predicates matters. Thus, the following expressions are not the same:

`chapter[example][2]`
: Selects the second `<chapter>` that includes `<example>` elements

`chapter[2][example]`
: Selects the second `<chapter>` element if it includes at least one `<example>` element

An expression can include logical or comparison operators. The following operators are available:

Operator	Meaning
`or`	Logical or
`and`	Logical and
`not()`	Negation
`= !=`	Equal to and different from
`< <=`	Less than and less than or equal to
`> >=`	More than and more than or equal to

The character < must be entered as < in expressions. Parentheses may be used for grouping. For example:

chapter[@title = 'XPath']
: Selects <chapter> elements where the title attribute has the value XPath

chapter[position() < 3]
: Selects the first two <chapter> elements

chapter[position() != last()]
: Selects <chapter> elements that are not in the last position

chapter[section/@title='examples' or subsection/@title='examples']
: Selects <chapter> elements that include <section> or <subsection> elements with the title attribute set to examples

XPath also defines operators that act on numbers. The numeric operators are +, -, *, div (division of real numbers), and mod (modulo).

Functions

In the previous examples we saw such XPath functions as position() and not(). XPath defines four basic types of functions that return: booleans (true or false), numbers (real numbers), strings (strings of characters), and node-sets. The functions are grouped based on the datatypes they act upon.

The following functions deal with node-sets (optional arguments are followed by a question mark):

last()
: Returns the total number of nodes of which the context node is a part

position()
: Returns a number that is the position of the context node (in document order or after sorting)

`count(node-set)`
: Returns the number of nodes contained in the specified *node-set*

`id(name)`
: Returns the node with the identifier *name*

`local-name([node-set])`
: Returns a string that is the name (without the namespace) of the first node in document order of the *node-set*, or the context-node, if the argument is omitted

`namespace-uri([node-set])`
: Returns a string that is the URI for the namespace of the first node in document order of the *node-set*, or the context node, if the argument is omitted

`name([node-set])`
: Returns a string that is the full name (with namespace) of the first node in document order of the *node-set*, or the context node, if the argument is omitted

The following functions deal with strings:

`string(object)`
: Converts its argument *object*, which can be of any type, to a string.

`concat(str1, str2, ...)`
: Returns the concatenation of its arguments.

`starts-with(str1, str2)`
: Returns `true` if the first argument string (*str1*) starts with the second argument string (*str2*).

`contains(str1, str2)`
: Returns `true` if the first argument string (*str1*) contains the second argument string (*str2*).

`substring-before (str1, str2)`
: Returns the substring of the first argument string (*str1*) that precedes the first occurrence of the second argument string (*str2*).

`substring-after (`*`str1, str2`*`)`
: Returns the substring of the first argument string (*`str1`*) that follows the first occurrence of the second argument string (*`str2`*).

`substring(`*`str, num`*`[, `*`length`*`])`
: Returns the substring of the first argument (*`str`*) starting at the position specified by the second argument (*`num`*) with the *`length`* specified in the third. If the third argument is not specified, the substring continues to the end of the string.

`string-length(`*`str`*`)`
: Returns the number of characters in the string.

`normalize-space(`*`str`*`)`
: Returns the argument string with whitespace normalized by stripping any leading and trailing whitespace and replacing sequences of whitespace characters by a single space.

`translate(`*`str1, str2, str3`*`)`
: Returns the first argument string (*`str1`*) with occurrences of characters in the second argument string (*`str2`*) replaced by the character at the corresponding position in the third argument string (*`str3`*).

The following functions deal with boolean operations:

`boolean(`*`object`*`)`
: Converts its argument (*`object`*), which can be of any type, to a boolean

`not(`*`boolean`*`)`
: Returns `true` if its argument evaluates as false

`true()`
: Returns `true`

`false()`
: Returns `false`

`lang(`*`str`*`)`
: Returns `true` if the language of the document (or the closest ancestor indicating the language) is the language passed in the argument (*`str`*)

The following functions deal with numbers:

`number([`*`obj`*`])`
: Converts its argument (*`obj`*), which can be of any type, to a number (using the context node if the argument is omitted.)

`sum(`*`node-set`*`)`
: Returns the sum of the result of converting every node in the *`node-set`* to a number. If any node is not a number, the function returns `NaN` (not a number).

`floor(`*`num`*`)`
: Returns the largest integer that is not greater than the argument (*`num`*).

`ceiling(`*`num`*`)`
: Returns the smallest integer that is not less than the argument (*`num`*).

`round(`*`num`*`)`
: Returns the integer that is closest to the argument (*`num`*).

These functions can be used not only in XPath expressions, but in XSLT elements as well. For example, to count the number of sections in a text, we could add the following to a stylesheet:

```
<xsl:text>The number of sections is </xsl:text>
<xsl:value-of select="count(//section)"/>
```

Additional XSLT Functions and Types

XSLT defines additional functionality for its own needs. One feature is a new datatype (in addition to the four datatypes defined by XPath): the *result tree fragment*. This datatype is comparable to a node-set, except that its nodes are in a tree rather than an unorganized collection. All the operations that are permitted for node-sets are permitted for tree fragments. However, you cannot use the `/`, `//`, or `[ ]` operators on result tree fragments.

XSLT also defines additional functions:

`document(`*`obj`*`[, `*`node-set`*`])`
: Returns a node-set that comprises the document whose URI (related to the second, optional argument) was passed as the first argument ***`obj`***. If the second argument is omitted, the context node is used.

`key(`*`str`*`, `*`obj`*`)`
: Returns the node-set of the nodes keyed by ***`obj`*** in the key named ***`str`*** (see the section "XSLT Elements" for an example).

`format-number(`*`num`*`, `*`str1`*`[, `*`str2`*`])`
: Returns a string containing the formatted value of ***`num`***, according to the format-pattern string in ***`str1`*** and the decimal-format string in ***`str2`*** (or the default decimal-format if there is no third argument).

`current()`
: Returns the current node.

`unparsed-entity-uri(`*`str`*`)`
: Returns the URI of the unparsed entity given by ***`str`***.

`generate-id(`*`node-set`*`)`
: Generates a unique `ID` for the first node in the given *`node-set`*.

`system-property(`*`str`*`)`
: Returns the value of the system property passed as a string *`str`*. The system properties are: `xsl:version` (the version of XSLT implemented by the processor), `xsl:vendor` (a string identifying the vendor of the XSL processor), and `xsl:vendor-url` (the vendor's URL).

XPointer and XLink

The final pieces of XML we cover are XPointer and XLink. These are separate standards in the XML family dedicated to working with XML links. Before we delve into them, however, we should warn you that the standards described here are not final as of publication time.

It's important to remember that an XML link is only an *assertion* of a relationship between pieces of documents; how the link is actually presented to a user depends on a number of factors, including the application processing the XML document.

Unique Identifiers

To create a link, we must first have a labeling scheme for XML elements. One way to do this is to assign an identifier to specific elements we want to reference using an `ID` attribute:

```
<paragraph id="attack">
Suddenly the skies were filled with aircraft.
</paragraph>
```

You can think of `ID`s in XML documents as street addresses: they provide a unique identifier for an element within a document. However, just as there might be an identical address in a different city, an element in a different document might have the same `ID`. Consequently, you can tie together an `ID` with the document's URI, as shown here:

```
http://www.oreilly.com/documents/story.xml#attack
```

The combination of a document's URI and an element's `ID` should uniquely identify that element throughout the universe. Remember that an `ID` attribute does not need to be named `id`, as shown in the first example. You can name it anything you want, as long as you define it as an XML `ID` in the document's DTD. (However, using `id` is preferred in the event that the XML processor does not read the DTD.)

Should you give an ID to every element in your documents? No. Odds are that most elements will never be referenced. It's best to place IDs on items that a reader would want to refer to later, such as chapter and section divisions, as well as important items, such as term definitions.

ID References

The easiest way to refer to an ID attribute is with an ID reference, or IDREF. Consider this example:

```
<?xml version="1.0" standalone="yes"?>
<DOCTYPE document [
   <!ELEMENT document (employee*)>
   <!ELEMENT employee (#PCDATA)>
   <!ATTLIST employee empnumber ID #REQUIRED>
   <!ATTLIST employee boss IDREF #IMPLIED>
]>
<employee empnumber="emp123">Jay</employee>
<employee empnumber="emp124">Kay</employee>
<employee empnumber="emp125" boss="emp123">Frank</employee>
<employee empnumber="emp126" boss="emp124">Hank</employee>
```

As with ID attributes, an IDREF is typically declared in the DTD. However, if you're in an environment where the processor might not read the DTD, you should call your ID references IDREF.

The chief benefit of using an IDREF is that a validating parser can ensure that every one points to an actual element; unlike other forms of linking, an IDREF is guaranteed to refer to something within the current document.

As we mentioned earlier, the IDREF only asserts a relationship of some sort; the stylesheet and the browser will determine what is to be done with it. If the referring element has some content, it might become a link to the target. But if the referring element is empty, the stylesheet might instruct the browser to perform some other action.

As for the linking behavior, remember that in HTML a link can point to an entire document (which the browser will download and display, positioned at the top) or to a specific location in a document (which the browser will display, usually positioned with that point at the top of the screen). However, linking changes drastically in XML. What does it mean to have a link to an entire element, which might be a paragraph (or smaller) or an entire group of chapters? The XML application attempts some kind of guess, but the display is best controlled by the stylesheet. For now, it's best to simply make a link as meaningful as you can.

XPointer

XPointer is designed to resolve the problem of locating an element or range of elements in an XML document. It is possible to do this in HTML if the element is referenced by an `<a name="name">` tag. Here, a link is made for the section of the document using the `<a href="url#name">` tag.

Fragment-identifier syntax

As we saw earlier, XML has this type of functionality through its unique identifiers. It is possible to locate an element with an identifier using a link such as the following:

```
document.xml#identifier
```

where ***identifier*** is a valid XPointer fragment identifier. However, this form is a simplification that is tolerated for compatibility with previous versions. The most common syntax for an XPointer fragment identifier is:

```
document.xml#xpointer(xpath)
```

Here *xpath* is an expression consistent with the XPath specification. It is the right thing to do in this case because it can be used to locate a node-set within a document. The link ***document.xml#identifier*** can be rewritten as:

```
document.xml#xpointer(id("identifier"))
```

There is a third possible form made up of a whole number separated by slashes. Each whole number selects an *n*th child from its predecessor in the expression.

Several fragment identifiers can be combined by placing them one after the other. For example:

```
document.xml#xpointer(...)xpointer(...)...
```

The application must evaluate the fragments, from left to right, and use the first valid fragment. This functionality is useful for two reasons:

- It offers several solutions, the first of which is based on suppositions that may prove to be false (and produce an error). For example, we can try to locate a fragment in a document using an identifier, then (if no `ID` was defined) using the attribute value with the name `id`. We would write the fragment:

  ```
  xpointer(id("conclusion"))xpointer(//*[@id='conclusion'])
  ```

- It also allows for future specifications. If an XPointer application encounters an expression that does not begin with `xpointer`, it will simply ignore it and move on to the next expression.

As we mentioned earlier, the XPointer application is responsible for link rendering, but it is also responsible for error handling. If the link's URL is wrong or if the fragment identifier is not valid, it is up to the application to manage the situation (by displaying an error message, for example).

XPointer datatypes

Earlier we showed you how to locate an XML node within a document. XPointer goes even further by defining the *point*, *range*, and *position* (location) types:

Point
: Can precede or follow a node (point of type `node`) or a character (thus, a point of type `character`).

Range

Is defined as the content of a document between two points (where the starting point cannot be located after the ending point within a document). A range cannot be reduced to a set of nodes and characters because it can include fragments of the former.

Position

Is a generalized concept of the node. It can be a node, a point, or a range.

Equipped with these new datatypes, XPointer can set out to locate a resource in an XML document.

Manipulation of points, ranges, and positions

A range is defined using the `to` operator. This operator is enclosed in starting points (to the left) and ending points (to the right). The second point is calculated using the first point as a reference. For example, to make a range from the beginning of the first paragraph to the end of the last paragraph in a section where the `ID` is `XPointer`, you would write:

```
xpointer(id("XPointer")/para[1] to
id("XPointer")/para[last()])
```

or:

```
xpointer(id("XPointer")/para[1] to
following-sibling::para[last()])
```

A range defined this way may be compared with the selection a user can make in a document with a mouse.

Naturally, XPointer also has functions to manipulate points and ranges. The available functions are:

`string-range(`*`positions`*`, `*`string`*`[, `*`offset`*`][, `*`length`*`])`

This function can be used to search for strings in a document and return a set of positions where they appear. The first argument is an XPath expression—a set of positions where the search must take place. The second is the string being searched. To search for the string `XML` in

`<chapter>` elements where the `title` attribute is `XPointer`, we would write the expression:

```
string-range(//chapter[@title='XPointer'], "XML")
```

To index the word `XML` by pointing to the first occurrence of the word in an element such as `<para>`, use the following expression:

```
string-range(//para, "XML")[1]
```

This function takes two other optional arguments. The third argument, ***offset***, is a number that indicates the first character to be included in the result range offset from the beginning of the string searched for. The fourth argument, ***length***, gives the length of the result range. By default, ***offset*** has a value of 1, thus the result range begins before the first character in the string. ***length*** has a default value such that the result range covers the entire string searched.

`range(`*`positions`*`)`
: This function takes an XPath expression and returns a set of ranges (a location set) where each includes the positions passed as parameters. It can be used to convert a set of positions (which may be nodes) to a set comprising ranges only.

`range-inside(`*`positions`*`)`
: This function takes an XPath expression and returns a set of ranges (a location set) for each of the positions passed as arguments.

`start-point(`*`positions`*`)`
: This function takes an XPath expression and returns the starting point of the range for each of the positions passed as arguments. The result is a set of points.

`end-point(`*`positions`*`)`
: This function takes an XPath expression and returns the end point of the range for each of the positions passed as arguments. The result is a set of points.

`here()`
: This function is defined only within an XML document. It returns a unique position comprising the element containing the XPointer expression or the attribute that contains it.

`origin()`
: This function can be used only for links triggered by the user. It returns the element's position to the original link.

XLink

Now that we know about XPointer, let's take a look at some inline links:

```
<?xml version="1.0"?>
<simpledoc xmlns:xlink="http://www.w3.org/1999/xlink">
<title>An XLink Demonstration</title>
<section id="target-section">
   <para>This is a paragraph in the first section.</para>
   <para>More information about XLink can be found at
      <reference xlink:type="simple"
      xlink:href="http://www.w3.org">
      the W3C
      </reference>.
   </para>
</section>
<section id="origin-section">
   <para>
   This is a paragraph in the second section.
   </para>
   <para>
   You should go read
      <reference xlink:type="simple"
      xlink:href="#target-section">
      the first section
      </reference>
   first.
   </para>
</section>
</simpledoc>
```

The first link states that the text "the W3C" is linked to the URL *http://www.w3.org*. How does the browser know? Simple.

An HTML browser knows that every `<a>` element is a link because the browser has to handle only one document type. In XML, you can make up your own element type names, so the browser needs some way of identifying links.

XLink provides the `xlink:type` attribute for link identification. A browser knows it has found a simple link when any element sets the `xlink:type` attribute to a value of `simple`. A simple link is like a link in HTML—one-way and beginning at the point in the document where it occurs. (In fact, HTML links can be recast as XLinks with minimal effort.) In other words, the content of the link element can be selected for traversal at the other end. Returning to the source document is left to the browser.

Once an XLink processor has found a simple link, it looks for other attributes that it knows:

`xlink:href`
: This attribute is deliberately named to be familiar to anyone who's used the Web before. Its value is the URI of the other end of the link; it can refer to an entire document or to a point or element within that document. If the target is in an XML document, the fragment part of the URI is an XPointer.

  This attribute must be specified, since without it, the link is meaningless. It is an error not to include it.

`xlink:role`
: This describes the nature of the object at the other end of the link. XLink doesn't predefine any roles; you might use a small set to distinguish different types of links in your documents, such as cross-references, additional reading, and contact information. A stylesheet might take a different action (such as presenting the link in a different color) based on the role, but the application won't do anything automatically.

`xlink:title`
: A title for the resource at the other end of the link can be provided, identical to HTML's `title` attribute for the `<a>` element. A GUI browser might display the title as a tool tip; an aural browser might read the title when the user pauses at the link before selecting it. A stylesheet might also make use of the information, perhaps to build a list of references for a document.

`xlink:show`
: This attribute suggests what to do when the link is traversed. It can take the following values:

    `embed`
    : The content at the other end of the link should be retrieved and displayed where the link is. An example of this behavior in HTML is the `<img>` element, whose target is usually displayed within the document.

    `replace`
    : When the link is activated, the browser should replace the current view with a view of the resource targeted by the link. This is what happens with the `<a>` element in HTML: the new page replaces the current one.

    `new`
    : The browser should somehow create a new context, if possible, such as opening a new window.

    `other`
    : This value specifies behavior that isn't described by the other values. It is up to the application to determine how to display the link.

    `none`
    : This specifies no behavior.

    You do not need to give a value for this attribute. Remember that a link primarily *asserts* a relationship between data; behavior is best left to a stylesheet. So unless the behavior is paramount (as it might be in some cases of `embed`, it is best not to use this attribute.

`xlink:actuate`
: The second of the behavioral attributes specifies when the link should be activated. It can take the following values:

  `onRequest`
  : The application waits until the user requests that the link be followed, as the `<a>` element in HTML does.

  `onLoad`
  : The link should be followed immediately when it is encountered by the application; this is what most HTML browsers do with `<img>` elements, unless the user has turned off image loading.

  `other`
  : The link is activated by other means, not specified by XLink. This is usually defined by other markup in the document.

  `none`
  : This indicates no information about the activation of the link and may be used when the link has no current meaningful target or action.

Building Extended Links

XLink has much more to offer, including links to multiple documents and links between disparate documents (where the XML document creating the links does not even contain any links).

Extended links

An XLink application recognizes extended links by the presence of an `xlink:type="extended"` attribute that distinguishes it from a simple link (such as those used in HTML). An extended link may have semantic attributes (`xlink:role` and `xlink:title`) that function just as they do for a simple link.

In addition, an extended link may be one of four types as defined by its `xlink:type="type"` attribute:

`resource`
: Supplies the local resource for the link (generally the text used to materialize the link)

`locator`
: Supplies a URI for the remote document participating in the link

`arc`
: Supplies a description of the potential paths among the documents participating in the extended link

`title`
: Supplies a label for the link

Consider this example of an extended link supplying an XML bibliography:

```
<biblio xlink:type="extended">
   <text xlink:type="resource"
      xlink:role="text">XML Bibliography</text>
   <book xlink:type="locator" xlink:role="book"
      xlink:href="xmlgf.xml"
         xlink:title="XML Pocket Reference"/>
   <book xlink:type="locator" xlink:role="book"
      xlink:href="lxml.xml"
         xlink:title="Learning XML"/>
   <author xlink:type="locator" xlink:role="author"
      xlink:href="robert-eckstein.xml"
         xlink:title="Robert Eckstein"/>
   <author xlink:type="locator" xlink:role="author"
      xlink:href="erik-ray.xml"
         xlink:title="Erik Ray"/>
   <arc xlink:type="arc"/>
</biblio>
```

The extended link will probably be represented graphically as a menu with an entry for each element, except for the last one (`arc`), which has no graphical representation. However, the graphical representation of the link is the application's responsibility. Let's look at the role of each of the elements.

Resource elements

Resource elements, which include the `xlink:type="resource"` attribute, define a local resource that participates in a link. An extended link that includes a resource is considered inline because the file in which it is found participates in a link. A link that has no resource is called out-of-line.

XLink applications use the following attributes:

Attribute	Description
`xlink:type`	`resource` (fixed value)
`xlink:role`	Role of this resource in the link (used by arcs)
`xlink:title`	Text used by the XLink application to represent this resource

In our example, the `<text>` element supplies the text to be displayed to represent the link.

Locator elements

Locator elements have the `xlink:type="locator"` attribute and use a URI to point to a remote resource. XLink applications use the following locator attributes:

Attribute	Description
`xlink:type`	`locator` (fixed value)
`xlink:href`	URI of the resource pointed to
`xlink:role`	Role resource pointed to (used by arcs)
`xlink:title`	Text the XLink application uses to graphically represent the resource

In our example, we use two kinds of locators: those with a role of `book` that point to documents describing publications, and those with a role of `author` that point to a biography. Here, the role is important because it tells the XLink application the potential traversals among resources.

Arc elements

Arc elements have the `xlink:type="arc"` attribute and determine the potential traversals among resources, as well as the behavior of the XLink application during such traversals. Arc elements may be represented as arrows in a diagram, linking resources that participate in an extended link.

XLink applications use the following arc attributes:

Attribute	Description
`xlink:type`	`arc` (fixed value)
`xlink:from`	Indicates the role of the resource of the originating arc
`xlink:to`	Indicates the role of the resource of the destination arc
`xlink:show`	`new`, `replace`, `embed`, `other`, or `none`: tells the XLink application how to display the resource to which the arc is pointing
`xlink:actuate`	`onLoad`, `onRequest`, `other`, or `none`: tells the XLink application the circumstances under which the traversal is made
`xlink:arcrole`	Role of the arc
`xlink:title`	Text that may be used to represent the arc

The values of the `xlink:show` and `xlink:actuate` attributes have the same meaning as they do with simple links.

Let's go back to our example of the bibliography, where we could define the following arc:

```
<arc xlink:from="text" xlink:to="book"
   xlink:show="new" xlink:actuate="onRequest"/>
```

The arc creates a link from the text displayed by the navigator (a resource where the role is `text`) to the descriptive page from the book (remote resource where the role is `book`). It also indicates that the page must be displayed in a new window (`xlink:show="new"`) when the user clicks the mouse button (`xlink:actuate="onRequest"`).

To include the author's biography in the card for the book, we will define the following arc:

```
<arc xlink:from="book" xlink:to="author"
   xlink:show="embed" xlink:actuate="onLoad"/>
```

`xlink:show="embed"` indicates that the destination of the arc (the biography) must be included in the card for the book (origin of the arc) and that the destination must be included when the book page is loaded (`xlink:actuate="onLoad"`).

Finally, we need to indicate that the absence of the `xlink:from` or `xlink:to` attribute indicates that the origin or destination of the arc corresponds to all the roles defined in the link. Thus, the arc in our example (`<arc xlink:type="arc"/>`) authorizes all the traversals possible among the resources of the extended link.

Title elements

Elements with a type of `<title>` tell the XLink application the title of the extended link. This element is needed when you want titles to have markers (for example, to put the text in bold) or if you want to provide titles in multiple languages. A `<title>` element must have the `xlink:type="title"` attribute.

As there may be a large number of attributes for the elements participating in an extended link, we recommend using the default values in the DTD. This eliminates the need to include fixed-value attributes for an element.

For example, because the `xlink:type` attribute of the `<biblio>` element always has `extended` as the value, we could declare the `<biblio>` element in the DTD as follows:

```
<!ELEMENT biblio (text, book+, author+, arc+)>
<!ATTLIST biblio xlink:type (extended) #FIXED "extended">
```

We would not need to indicate the type, and if we proceed the same way for the other elements in the extended link, we could write the following link:

```
<biblio>
   <text>XML Bibliography</text>
   <book xlink:href="xmlgf.xml"
      xlink:title="XML Pocket Reference"/>
   <book xlink:href="lxml.xml"
      xlink:title="Learning XML"/>
   <author xlink:href="robert-eckstein.xml"
      xlink:title="Robert Eckstein"/>
   <author xlink:href="erik-ray.xml"
      xlink:title="Erik Ray"/>
   <arc/>
</biblio>
```

By limiting ourselves to the strict minimum (attributes where the value is fixed do not need to be written), we gain readability.

Linkbases

As indicated earlier, an extended link with no resource-type element (local resource) is described as being out-of-line. Therefore, this type of link is not defined in any files to which it points. It may be convenient to regroup extended links in XML files called *linkbases*.

This raises the question as to the location of such XML files. If we have no way of finding the linkbases associated with a given file (not provided in the W3C specification), we must indicate the URI in one of the files participating in the link. This is possible thanks to the `xlink:role` attribute with the value `xlink:extended-linkset`.

The XLink application recognizes the attribute and can look for the associated linkbase where the URI is indicated by the `xlink:href` attribute. For example, to link the linkbase of the URI *linkbase.xml* to an XML file, we could use an element with the following syntax:

```
<linkbase>
<uri xlink:role="XLink:extended-linkset"
   xlink:href="linkbase.xml"/>
</linkbase>
```

We can indicate as many linkbases in a file as we want. A linkbase can itself contain a reference to another linkbase. It is up to the XLink application to manage circular references and limit the depth of the search for linkbases.

XBase

XBase is a W3C specification currently in development. XBase can be used to change the base of URIs in an XML document (which, by default, is the document's directory). XLink processors take XBase into consideration in order to manage URIs, using the `xml:base="URI"` attribute as follows:

```
<base xml:base="http://www.oreilly.com/bdl/"/>
<linkbase>
   <uri xlink:role="xlink:extended-linkset"
       xlink:href="linkbase.xml"/>
</linkbase>
```

The *linkbase.xml* linkbase is searched for in the *http://www.oreilly.com/bdl/* directory, not in the directory of the document where the request was made to load the linkbase.

Loading of the base continues in the nodes that descend from the node in which the base is defined (this is the same behavior as the `xml:lang` and `xml:space` attributes).

Other Titles Available from O'Reilly

XML

XML in a Nutshell, 2nd Edition

By Elliotte Rusty Harold & W. Scott Means
1st Edition December 2000
400 pages, ISBN 0-596-00058-8

XSLT Cookbook

By Sal Mangano
1st Edition December 2002
670 pages, ISBN 0-596-00372-2

Learning XML

By Erik T. Ray with Christopher R. Maden
1st Edition January 2001
368 pages, ISBN 0-596-00046-4

XML Schema

By Eric van der Vlist
1st Edition June 2002
400 pages, 0-596-00252-1

XSLT

By Doug Tidwell
1st Edition August 2001
473 pages, ISBN 0-596-00053-7

Java & XML, 2nd Edition

By Brett McLaughlin
2nd Edition September 2001
528 pages, ISBN 0-596-00197-5

SAX2

By David Brownell
1st Edition January 2002
240 pages, ISBN 0-596-00237-8

SVG Essentials

By J. David Eisenberg
1st Edition, February 2002
368 pages, ISBN 0-596-00223-8

Programming Jabber

By DJ Adams
1st Edition January 2002
480 pages, ISBN 0-596-00202-5

Web Services Essentials

By Ethan Cerami
1st Edition February 2002
304 pages, ISBN 0-596-00224-6

Content Syndication with RSS

By Ben Hammersley
1st Edition March 2003
216 pages, ISBN 0-596-00383-8

Programming Web Services with SOAP

By James Snell, Doug Tidwell & Pavel Kulchenko
1st Edition December 2001
264 pages, ISBN 0-596-00095-2

XSL-FO

By Dave Pawson
1st Edition August 2002
282 pages, ISBN 0-596-00355-2

The XML CD Bookshelf

By O'Reilly & Associates, Inc.
Version 1.0 November 2002
640 pages, ISBN 0-596-00335-8

Perl & XML

By Erik T. Ray & Jason McIntosh
1st Edition April 2002
216 pages, ISBN 0-596-00205-X

XPath and XPointer

By John E. Simpson
1st Edition August 2002
208 pages, ISBN 0-596-00291-2

Java and XSLT

By Eric M. Burke
1st Edition September 2001
528 pages, ISBN 0-596-00143-6

Python & XML

By Christopher A. Jones & Fred Drake
1st Edition December 2001
378 pages, ISBN 0-596-00128-2